Quick Serv

A Guide for Repair Shop Management In New Car Dealerships

Patrick W. Emmett

DEDICATION

I dedicate this book to the many automobile Dealers that I have met over the years and the men and women in the car manufacturing business with whom I have worked. They are dedicated professionals who are devoted to providing the best possible service to their customers.

CONTENTS

Patrick W. Emmett

CONTENTS (CONTINUED)

- Hours of Operation
- Quick Service Phones
- Uniforms
- Advertising and Marketing
- Personalization/Accessories
- Hiring the Right People
- Technicians and Pay Plans
- Other Opportunities for Quick Service
- Measuring Quick Service Performance

Patrick W. Emmett

Disclaimer Message:

The opinions and conclusions that I have presented in these pages are my own, based on many years of observation in the automotive industry. I make no claims of fact concerning statements or warrants made about the Automobile Manufacturers or Vendors mentioned or any programs that they may or may not support or their business mission. Any Dealer examples that I may have listed, are for demonstration purposes only and do not characterize or represent any specific dealers. All of the content in this book is my own. My intention is not to offend but rather enlighten anyone who is interested in creating a quick service opportunity in their business.

ACKNOWLEDGMENTS

I am a humble student of automobile dealership fixed operations. My wish is to share what I know in an effort to better serve our customer base, to keep our Dealers healthy and automobile manufacturers in the business of making vehicles.

In particular, I would like to acknowledge:

Alan Mulally & Bill Ford for your kind words concerning my first book.

I learn something new every time I walk through a dealership's doors.

I hope we all can keep an open perspective as we continue to learn.

PROLOGUE

If you are a car Dealer, when do you begin to listen to what your customers are telling you? When do you make the decision to change the way you are doing business? Is quick service in a car dealership an oxymoron?

The purpose of this book is to provide car Dealers with information about segmenting quick service in their service departments into a separate profit center. Customers are demanding and they deserve an oil change in 30 minutes or less. They deserve to have their tires changed while they wait. They need options and choices about how much they want to spend on light repairs, such as a brake job. They want an honest and fair assessment of what it will take to fix their vehicles. Service like this is readily available in the after-market. If you, as a car Dealer, do not provide excellent service to your customers, your competition will.

I have spent many years traveling from coast to coast counseling and working with car Dealers to help them improve their service department operations and customer satisfaction indexes. I have seen the positive results that come from listening to your customers' needs.

Every dealership is unique. Location, franchise, facility footprint, customer mix and who you have employed all can make a difference in how you take care of your customers once they have purchased a vehicle from you. Keep in mind that there are no single, simple answers that will work for all Dealers.

My book, Quick Serv, will present several options for you to consider. The information in these pages is meant to inform, not make a decision for you. Over the years I have been instrumental in guiding car Dealers through the decision making process of segmenting quick service from their main production shops. Some Dealers have chosen to add 14 bay stand alone facilities near their main dealership while others have opted to simply convert two or three bays of their existing operation into a better work flow model. Somewhere in between there is an answer for you. One thing is for sure, in today's competitive market you must be better than the other guy in order to keep your customers coming back to you.

Now is the best possible time to be making a decision about expanding your dealership's service operation. Service is working for most Dealers. They make a very good gross profit from labor and parts sales. The time is ripe to capitalize on this money maker. Right now, interest rates are as low as they have been for some time. Construction costs will only go up in the future. Currently, there is a flood of good talent in the marketplace to help you run a new quick service center. Finally, the quickest way to increase Fixed Coverage is to add a new profit center to the fixed operations department.

Before you know where you are going, you should at least know how you got to where you are at. This book will review our business from several angles and you will read some opinions that you may not agree with. Just keep an open mind and use what works for you.

As a savvy business person, you recognize opportunity when you see it. Just like in tennis, you have to be ready for anything that comes at you. The ball is in your court, your have to be ready for that Quick Serv when the time comes.

CHAPTER 1

THE AUTOMOTIVE BUSINESS CLIMATE

Who could have ever forecast the series of events that took place from August 2008 to May of 2009?

We have seen huge losses on Wall Street, banks failing, the roots of our financial system turned upside down and the bankruptcy of Chrysler and General Motors. Financial institutions that we have trusted with our money have been accused of bundling and selling derivatives. Derivatives in essence, are a collection of gambling risks or bets as to how much mortgage debt would increase or fall. The amount of mortgage derivatives represented in these bundles exceeded by several fold the debt load of the mortgages themselves. This structure was the heart and sole of the sub-prime money lending industry. It was all a house of cards and everything came collapsing down early in 2008.

At the time, money was lent to large developers with little or no collateral for huge real estate developments and condominium projects in several states; California, Florida and Nevada in particular. Several smaller banks made back-room deals to get into the game.

Sweetheart deals were made for friends and family members. Everyone was betting on the increase in property values and a cash rich economy. Real estate values skyrocketed.

Pension Fund managers and institutional investors moved money out of their stock portfolios, to invest with Hedge Fund salesmen. They in turn, promised an incredible return-on-investments. They all wanted to be heroes.

Then something terrible happened. The people who borrowed the money failed to pay it back. The sub-prime customers who were high risk to start with either paid late or didn't pay at all on mortgage loans. The huge developers who were building all of the high-priced real-estate on speculation suddenly had to fill the space with anyone they could put into the property. They did so at a loss, and they too defaulted on their loans. Eventually, many of the developers went bankrupt leaving the lenders holding property that was often way overvalued.

Banks who had made sub-prime loans found their borrowers in default. The banking industry suddenly had no cash. Investment bankers who make a reputation out of solid business decisions were suddenly at risk because of loaning billions to support the derivative gold rush. The banks still had the property as collateral at a fraction of the loaned amount but the derivatives were actually a bet on how much the value of the mortgages would gain or loose over time. When the mortgages failed, the derivatives had no foundation or collateral to fall back on. The money simply wasn't there.

In a panic to cover their losses on the gambled derivatives, banks, investment and Pension Fund managers quickly sold stocks from their stock portfolio's, dumping what they could onto the market to recover what cash they could. This action caused a run on the sale of stocks which literally crashed their value in the market place even more.

Economists and soothsayers all predicted an Armageddon of economic disaster. In a rush, US Secretary Paulson petitioned Congress and the Bush Administration. They all agreed to dump $700 billion dollars from the US treasury into the banking system to keep our economy afloat. Public appeals were made by both political parties, the president made an urgent plea. There was very little debate on the subject. The money was appropriated with very few strings attached and not much oversight or what appeared to be forethought.

The country was in shock. No one could believe this had just happened. No one thought anything like this could happen to our economy. No one saw this coming. No one that is, except the US car Dealers and automobile manufacturers.

The car business is cyclical in nature. Customer buying decisions tend to ebb and flow with each technological innovation, fuel prices, car market incentives and the perceived general well-being of the average American. The sale of cars and trucks in this country is really a better economic indicator of how well the economy is doing for everyday people in this country than most other measurements. When people are employed and making money, vehicle sales go up. When farmers and ranchers are experiencing good market conditions, they buy new vehicles. All of this has a ripple effect on construction and commercial markets. When sales are down, people have a reason to not replace an aging vehicle. Sales drop when people are unemployed, underemployed, their business is suffering or crop prices are down. Fuel prices and interest rates play a roll but if people are not working, they are not buying. No car sales equal a weak economy.

Economists who forecast trends based on factory orders and the movements of electronic goods are a day late and many dollars short. People stop buying cars and trucks before the economists figure it out. Car Dealers know right away and they make adjustments to keep their businesses running.

Discussions in Dealer 20 Groups during the end of 2007 and throughout 2010 turned to conserving cash, methods of earning more gross profit, cutting expenses and reduction of personnel in order to survive. Dealers have been making adjustments for a falling economy long before TARP.

The economic boom for the car business lasted from roughly 1994 to 2007. This was a good long ride for the car business. In past years an up cycle may only last 5 to 7 years before another dip. Many Dealers became complacent. Some who got into the business late had never seen a down cycle. They did not realize that constant growth could come to an end.

For too many years, domestic automobile manufacturers have claimed that they were global entities. They were proud of their ability to go global. These companies built plants in other countries. In many cases they divested into businesses that were not related to the automobile manufacturing business at all. Collectively, they took their eye off of the most important automotive market, North America.

A case could be made that the North American economy is really grounded in the automobile industry. Consider the total impact of all jobs related to the automotive industry, such as automobile manufacturing jobs, both domestic and import. Think of all of the companies who supply the manufacturing segment. The transportation industry that moves the vehicles from place to place, an insurance industry that insures vehicles and business reliant on the car business, lending institutions on vehicle loans and floor plans, Mom and Pop repair shops, body shops, parts stores, gas stations, health insurance companies, the hospitality industry that relies on the trade of traveling marketing and sales personnel who move about the country, car rental companies, the car Dealers them selves and their employees. They all rely on a healthy automotive industry. The total cost of goods and services from the automotive industry would appear to exceed all other business models together with the possible exception of the US government.

Everyone thinks of the car business and they think cars. People who live in large cities are convinced that everyone should just buy small cars and the country will do better. The truth is, that in most of our country today, trucks are what make America work. Trucks are not a vanity purchase for most Americans. People in most of our country need these vehicles for their businesses, to haul things and to tow things. People buy a truck for many reasons beyond their business. They use them to take a boat to the lake, haul camping gear for the family and even help move their best friend. Excuse me, but you cannot haul a 22' ski boat to the lake with a 4 cylinder hybrid and take your family with you! That is why we have SUVs and pick-up trucks.

We recently faced an incredibly large snow storm in the Midwest and the Eastern part of our country. It was not the battery powered Prius that got people moving but rather the 4x4; 4Runner, Tundra, Silverado, Ram and F150's that the buying American public relies on.

Gas guzzler mentality aside, housewives want the security of all of that metal wrapped around them and their most precious possessions, their children, when they go to the grocery store or school in a snow storm. That is what the marketplace has asked for and what manufacturers have supplied a demanding public, not what someone else thinks they need to have.

When truck sales began to falter in 2007 and on into 2008, domestic companies like Ford, Chrysler and GM began to feel the pinch. Automobile manufacturer's profits were reliant on a robust truck business. When truck sales slipped so did profits. The sales decline also affected Toyota and Nissan who had both made sizable investments into United States plants that manufactured pick-up trucks. Truck sales plummeted, leaving those companies to reduce production and cut their losses.

Automobile manufacturers typically make lower profit margins on small gas saving entry level vehicles. These vehicles are an important part of delivering what the public wants in from a car company. Focusing on just building small entry level vehicles and ignoring the truck segment would be a formula for financial disaster for these car companies.

Chrysler is now a much smaller company now, as a result of their bankruptcy. They are relying on a strong domestic and import product line up with Fiat, while marketing vehicles through a much leaner Dealer body.

An interesting side note is that many Chrysler Dealers are now seeing the need to down-size their facilities. These Dealers had been in larger buildings doing a lot less volume than they once did. Recent changes have forced many Dealers to take a look at their real estate. Some Dealers have made swaps with some of the smaller import Dealers who were looking to expand.

Chrysler has made many strategic changes as well. There have been dramatic reductions in their field force, manufacturing and management staffs. More changes are forecasted as the company continues to change with the times.

General Motors has made great strides to pay of their TARP loan and their IPO has been characterized as very successful. They have made decisions to reduce the number of product lines and made painful decisions to trim their Dealer body. The company intends to survive and so they are going through many difficult cost cutting measures and personnel reduction plans.

Ford Motor Co. took major cuts a few years earlier than GM and Chrysler but they too have been watching manufacturing costs. They have trimmed production levels on certain models until demand rises.

Watching the declining economy, Ford set up lines of credit at low interest rates. They have relied on those lines of credit to keep them running during the economic slump. In the meantime, Ford made dramatic improvements in product quality and they began to advertise this fact aggressively and it helped!

During 2009 and 2010 Toyota, Honda and Nissan reined in North American production to meet demand. Toyota is even looking at a "back to the basics" business plan. Volkswagen, Mercedes and a collection of other imports that have assembly plants in North America have also slowed production to match the recession. Hopes are high for a robust recovery. Looking forward, it seems like the only thing that can hurt sustainable automotive growth is increasing fuel prices.

I recently spoke to a professor of economics in New Hampshire. He is convinced that gasoline prices will rise until they reach $7.00 per gallon and that they stay there. He told me that Americans will be forced to use more fuel efficient vehicles whether they like it or not. He further predicted that we will only have one or two domestic automobile manufacturers within 5 years. Americans will not be driving trucks in his vision of the future. I did not like what I heard and did not want to agree with him but there are a lot of people like him out there. If his prediction is true, the transport of goods and services will be severely curtailed and we will be facing a much different future than any of us would like to accept.

Today, fuel prices in this country fluctuate wildly. No one seems to have an adequate answer as to why. You hear that the price per barrel goes up and so do gasoline prices. Then you see the price per barrel go down and gas prices still staying up with all of us being told that the two are not connected.

We read in the press that the North American supply of crude oil is adequate and our reserves are high but gasoline prices still go up at the pump. Then just a suddenly, prices seem to topple down for no reason at all. Talking heads on television explain that some countries like Saudi Arabia and Venezuela control the flow of gasoline into our country and that affects gasoline prices at the pump. The irony is that when the price per barrel is low then domestic gasoline producers import more oil because it is cheaper than paying domestic oil producers to pump crude out of the ground in this country.

We import oil from Canada, Mexico, Saudi Arabia and South America every day. There is a movement afoot to avoid certain brands because the oil comes from countries where there are dictators. Yet some oil is purchased freely from other countries with kings and dictators and we are told that this is good for Americans. Everything about oil is a paradox.

We have all heard the mantra that "America needs to free it's self from dependence on foreign oil." A very simple truth is that most oil companies are multi-national in nature. Almost all oil, once it is pumped out of the ground, no matter where it comes from, is instantly considered a commodity and is sold in the world market to the highest bidder. Alaskan oil, more often than not, is shipped to Asia.

Venezuelan oil is produced by Petroleos de Venezuela (PDVSA). Chávez, the country's dictator, has threatened to cut-off shipments to the United States but the United States still exports between 30 to 50% of Venezuelan production. The Dutch island of Curasao has refineries that import crude from oil rich Venezuela and then it is marketed as Dutch Shell Oil in our country.

BP oil is a multinational company still primarily owned by British stockholders. Formerly known as British Petroleum they produce oil from all over the world. Oil fields in the North Sea, Canada, Southeast Asia and notably in the Gulf of Mexico are all owned and operated by British Petroleum. Oil comes into the US through oil giant the Saudi Arabian oil giant Aramco, which supplies oil to the United States through Standard Oil of California.

No matter where it comes from, oil when pumped out of the ground, is used to feed our need for gasoline and heating oil. We don't think about it, but the petrochemical industry to make plastic, is taking an even larger share of oil demand.

When we think of oil we think gasoline but plastics are a large part of the supply chain. The petrochemical industry is providing everything in our daily lives from the plastics used in our automobiles to the clothes on our backs to the pharmaceuticals in our bathroom vanity. There is very little that is manufactured today that does not have a petrochemical base to it. This is the wild card that affects our oil prices at the pump. Competition with new players on the block like China, India, Malaysia and Indonesia are very hungry for oil and plastics have a lot to do with their increasing demand. They take raw products, like oil and sell them back to us in the form of cheap trade goods.

Gasoline is still in high demand and if prices do reach $7.00 per gallon then the hue and cry for fuel economy in vehicles will be louder than ever. In defense of the automobile manufacturing segment, however, gasoline powered internal combustion engines are simply the most efficient power plants in the world to operate a vehicle at this time. Horsepower, torque and get-up and go are what consumers want and need. If there was a better, more economical method of providing power to move a vehicle then someone would have come up with the solution and it would be in production. The import companies are not bashful about bringing new technology into the North American market. If they had a better more economical way to do things we would have seen it by now.

If I had to place a bet, I would say that in the near future, we will see clean burning, fuel efficient diesel engines manufactured and used in all sizes of vehicles in this country. In the long run, more efficient use of natural gas and methane gas may provide a clean alternative to gasoline. We have vast reserves of natural gas but it is tightly regulated by the gas industry. There is an unlimited supply of frozen methane under the continental shelf surrounding the United States and none of it is being tapped. Burning frozen methane rather than having it escape into the atmosphere is a much friendlier solution for the future of our economy.

Batteries are a very expensive alternative. They are heavy thereby requiring more torque and horsepower. They represent an incredible bio-hazard for disposal after 7-10 years, perhaps a little longer with better technology. Batteries rely on an outside source of power such as a gas engine or plug into a wall for a re-charge thereby siphoning from another energy resource. Electric cars have a limited rage before recharging is required. Even Lithium-ion technology is showing slow progress for efficient battery packs to move vehicles.

Hydrogen fuel cells are great. They represent the long term future of automotive development. More cost efficient fuel cell technologies are being developed as we speak. GM has several fuel cell powered cars in California on a trial basis. They are a wonder. We still need an infrastructure to support Hydrogen fill up. There are just no panaceas for the immediate future.

Fuel prices will continue to fluctuate and rise, not necessarily due to free market demands. We cannot change this but we can look to the future of our car business and control what is in our power to change.

What all of this means is that for the short term there will be fewer cars on fewer lots to be sold to fewer customers by fewer Dealers. Eventually, North Americans will begin to rebuild their factories and focus on making things again. The unemployed will go back to work.

On a positive note, Americans are resilient. The combined knowledge and energy of our people will re-establish a sound economic base with customers buying new cars and trucks from forward thinking car Dealers.

CHAPTER 2

WHAT ARE YOU LOOKING FOR?

Imagine yourself in a room with many doors. All of them are locked. You look around in confusion at the many choices. Behind some doors there is a wonderful new opportunity waiting for you that could bring you wealth, happiness and satisfaction. Behind others lurk the pitfalls of poor planning and indecision. Then imagine that you were given a golden key that could unlock any door anytime you wanted to open one. Would you use it?

Many car Dealers are afraid of risk. They see the possibility of pitfalls that may be behind some of those doors and they choose to continue to do things the way they always have. As a Dealer, you currently hold that key. It is called change. You possess everything it takes to open any of those doors and face the challenges that lie beyond; all you need to do is embrace change.

In a leadership workshop that I have prepared, I discuss the concept of change and I ask Dealers and Managers what they need to do in order to accept change. I get a lot of answers but typically most Dealers and Managers feel that if they do not change the way they are currently doing business, that they will not be able to adapt to the shifting market trends that are affecting our business from every side. In other words, they may not be able to stay in business. They want to change, they just don't know how.

When I talk with Dealers they will ask me, "What is in the future for car Dealers?" I do not have that crystal ball but I can guess what direction automotive service departments are headed.

All automotive manufacturers are facing a major decrease in production which means fewer new car customers coming through single point dealership doors. As a result, we are seeing more and more multi-franchise consolidations taking place. There are more signs out in front of the typical dealership today. We are also seeing more Import franchises opening up in smaller markets.

We are seeing certified Technician labor rates that are exceeding our wildest imaginations while effective labor rates are not keeping pace in most shops. We see the ratio of domestic to import vehicle sales shifting at an alarming rate. That means that the average Technician must be proficient in not only a single car line, but several. With tough economic times, many customers are simply not bringing their vehicles, domestic or imported, in for regular maintenance. Even aftermarket vendors such as Jiffy Lube and Firestone are feeling the pinch. There are fewer certified Technicians filling the jobs of those who have left the field.

Over the years I have been very fortunate to have been associated with several talented and well informed individuals. I have learned much from these people and as an observer of this business and its trends I continue to learn and to view things in new ways. Every time I visit a dealership I learn something new. One thing that I have learned is that no one person or system has all of the answers.

Probably the most important thing to remember about doing things right in this business is that we need to keep a fresh perspective and we need to be prepared to adapt to changing market conditions. Really, there are no silver bullets and generally and there is nothing really new in our business. The only secret is; knowing when to make your move, how to get it done, by whom and following up on the changes once they are in place.

Some people are going to read this book and feel that they don't want to change. They have learned nothing new or they are already doing things better than the solutions I am putting forth. That's okay. Not all Dealers are created equal. Some are endowed with incredible resources and abilities to overcome any market conditions in their communities. Others are simply never going to be able to make the simple changes they need to make in order to survive for the long haul.

What I have learned, over the years, after visiting automotive dealerships, is that there are golden opportunities for growth and profit in just about every dealership. Often you don't have to look too far. There are books and training programs galore to help improve the fixed operations department. I can even recommend a few. The focus of this book is on how to maximize your customer pay business through the addition of a quick service opportunity to your business.

What ever you choose to do, the bottom line is that dealerships need to make a profit. If you are in business for any other reason, this book is probably not for you. When it comes to maximizing profits from a Parts and Service department and developing happy customers that want to return and do business with you, there are many choices. You have many doors to choose from but if you do nothing at all, you will have nothing to gain. You must be willing to embrace change.

CHAPTER 3

THE CAR BUSINESS TODAY

Car dealers for the most part, focus their energy talent and financial resources to growing their new and used vehicle departments. After all, that was why they came into this business, to sell cars. Daily attention is often riveted to the performance of the individuals who move vehicle sales numbers. Much of a dealership's working capital is generally invested into inventories of new and used cars and trucks. The Service, Parts and Body shop departments are a necessary but less visible part of many new car dealerships. Service operations are generally less important for used car Dealers.

The Service and Parts departments are generally called "fixed operations," "service" or euphemistically referred to as "the back end." Typically, the fixed operations department is entrusted to someone who has been around the dealership for a great many years. This is a person who frequently worked as a Technician earlier in his\her career. Through longevity and timing they wound up with the title of Service Manager or Fixed Operations Director.

A Service Manager will have several people reporting to them such as; a Shop Foreman, Warranty Clerk, and Service Advisors. Cashiers, Porters and Technicians are also direct reports to the Service Manager. The Service

Manager position is often balanced by a Parts Manager. Under this person you will find front and back Countermen, a Shipper/Receiver, Driver and still in many departments, a Data Entry Clerk. From dealership to dealership, there is very little difference in the jobs or job description.

The Parts Managers position appears to be in jeopardy. Automobile manufacturers have worked long and hard to relieve the Dealer from the burden of managing their own parts inventories. Manufacturers want to control the supply chain to better predict which parts to buy from their suppliers in an effort to control their cost. This leaves Dealers at their mercy as to which parts they may have on the shelf at any point in time.

Parts inventories often get out of hand with idle inventories that lock up Dealer investment capital, no matter who ordered it. Yet Dealers must trust that the parts department will do their best to make sure that Technicians will have the parts they need. Even though the Parts Manager position appears to be replaced by forces out of their control, Dealers still need the best possible gate keeper they can find to manage their investment on the shelves.

The dealerships' body shop is generally independent from the rest of the fixed operations department. They show up on the balance sheet each month with Parts and Service. Sometimes the Body Shop falls under the management of a Fixed Operations Director or Service Manager but typically these operations stand as their own profit center. A lot of dealerships still have a body shop on the property where the main dealership facility is located. Many Dealers are opting to recover that space near the physical plant of the dealership and move the body shop to another part of town where the real estate is cheaper.

In the not too distant past, body shops were very a desirable addition to new car facilities. Auto manufacturers kept the body shops busy with warranty body and paint work. Insurance companies were repairing and paining vehicles and customers would even paint their vehicles just to change the color.

Times have changed. The warranty body and paint business has evaporated. Car manufacturers are using different formulas and methods of applying paint at the factory. Insurance companies now often recommend the use of aftermarket and salvage parts to repair vehicles, leaving the new car parts department out of the loop. In today's world, not too many people are seeking vanity paint jobs any longer. It should also be noted that body shops are huge contributors to idle parts inventories on Dealer's shelves.

Traditional dealership service departments are under a lot of pressure. Changes in vehicles construction and market trends are occurring rapidly. The service department is seen as the bread and butter that will cover the dealership variable operations (front-end, vehicle sales) expense 100% in good times and more when business is down. This is called fixed coverage or service absorption, depending on which manufacturer you talk to. All of this has an affect on how business is being conducted. Innovative Dealers are looking at their service departments as a valuable resource for additional dealership profit, customer retention, and a source for new and used vehicle business.

Years ago, I performed a customer retention study at a dealership in Shreveport, LA. I presented the findings to the Dealer and pointed out that, while he had a great many new car customers returning to get a free first oil change, his retention of used vehicle customers was almost non-existent. The Dealer looked at me with shock and horror on his face and said, "Good God! Once the rubber is over the curb, I hope to never see those people again."

Thankfully, the day when you could sell a customer a vehicle and never see them again is gone. Yet there are still a few Dealers out there who make their name by new vehicle pump-out sales into other Dealers markets. These pump-out Dealers spend a lot of money on advertising and work on narrow profit margins to push new vehicle sales volume through their stores. A customer may buy once or even twice from a place like this but who will take care of them when they need service on that new vehicle purchase?

In today's world there are the internet buyers as well. They think of themselves as informed comparison shoppers. They have their vehicles sent to a delivering Dealer who gets paid a delivery fee. That Dealer made no profit on the deal and there is no relationship built between the customer and the Dealer. What will this customer do when they need service on that cyber purchased bargain? Just who is responsible for this customer when they do need service? This is a risky concept that these new car owners do not grasp.

We are really in a relationship business and customers would rather have the security of knowing who they are dealing with. This simple premise is what keeps customers coming back through car dealership doors. The good news for most Dealers is that customers are easily re-captured with excellent service. The old formulary that good customer service in the service department will sell cars, still rings true today.

If a Dealer did not sell the vehicle to a customer it is easy for their employees to think of these people as "visiting owners." It is a sad truth that customers may not receive a decent service experience because they failed to purchase from a servicing dealership. What many Service Advisors fail to take into consideration is that most customers are 2 to 4 car households and they all have extended families. There is excellent potential here for future car and service sales when treating the customer well can win them over for buying from you the next time or the potential to drive away a lot of extended business.

In today's market, most customers feel comfortable working with the same dealership again and again. They will ask for the same salesperson and prefer to return to the same service advisor that they have come to know. The import and luxury market has known this for years. In fact, some hi-line manufacturers like Mercedes Benz, require that rigid maintenance records are kept in order to keep the factory warranty in force. Customers who return again and again will forge an irrevocable relationship with their Dealer.

Toyota has been a leader by training customers to maintain their vehicles for lower cost of ownership and higher resale value. Customers are convinced that they will get the best possible service from their selling Dealer. Toyota, Honda and Nissan have won customer loyalty by keeping them coming back to the dealership for maintenance. Newcomers like Hyundai and Kia are doing the same with 5 year 100,000 mile warranties while drastically improving quality and delivering quality service.

The numbers vary, but loyalty is especially important for women consumers. This buying segment represents approximately 37% of new vehicle sales and about 48% of service sales. When polled, women stress the need to develop a relationship with the dealership and the people who work there. They want to be able to trust the people who work on their cars and they want honest advice delivered in a way that is not perceived as demeaning. They want to be recognized as well informed, decisive buyers of goods and services. They are not shy about going someplace else if they do not get treated with respect. More importunately, they do not mind telling everyone they know exactly how they feel. Any dealership that is not taking steps to pay special attention to their female customers has lost before they began.

In the service business it is harder to change perceptions than it is to maintain momentum. Once you get the customer to return to your dealership you still have to provide them with a positive service experience or else you loose them. Dealership personnel have to constantly be on their game to provide the best possible attention to customer's needs and expectations.

I worked with successful Dealers who have told me that they were in the business of providing a "surprise and delight experience" for customers. I thought this was a wonderful concept. They believed that "the customer should leave the dealership always feeling like they got something extra." Thinking for out of the box solutions can keep your customers coming back.

I have been told that process flow in New Car dealerships can sometimes best be described as controlled chaos. No matter how much we plan or prepare for things the unexpected always happens. For example, the day that you advertise for a service special is also the same day that your key service advisor is absent because his wife has just gone into pre-mature labor. Technicians go missing in action during the summer rush and in some markets it seems like a good idea to just close the shop during deer hunting season. We have a fun business and we can always expect the unexpected.

CHAPTER 4

SOME THOUGHTS ON THE CAR BUSINESS

New car Dealers today are challenged way beyond measure. The day when customers would just come to a car Dealer every 5 years and pick out a new vehicle are a thing of the past. The cycle is now 7-8 years. All automakers are seriously downsizing their field operations and manufacturing goals to match their forecasted US market share. We have already seen a major reduction in dealer franchises from coast to coast.

Despite the manufacturer's efforts to have larger single point dealerships, the trend seems to be leaning to more franchises under a single roof. Drive down the street. You will see more imported nameplates in domestic facilities and domestic nameplates in imported facilities than ever before. There will continue to be fewer Dealers in rural markets. Manufacturers simply do not want the expense of servicing low-end producers. It's a shame really; some of these businesses have held franchise in their families for generations. As consolidations continue in the coming years, there will be an increase of larger auto dealer groups on into the next decade.

An interesting observation of the consolidation trend is that large auto groups with several name plates have a lot of comprehensive statistical and demographic data of any given market place. They will know exactly what the customers are asking for in automotive products. They know by name plate, size, options and color what current demand is. In an interesting twist, large retail operations could be dictating what the manufacturers produce and deliver on a short turnaround basis in the future. Mega dealer groups could possibly be driving manufacturing cycles; down to price points and appointments. Volume could be king in this "tail wagging the dog" scenario. .

The future may even see Mega Groups contract with manufacturing facilities for the production of special boutique "branded" vehicle lines. This concept would be a complete reversal of the way automobile business has gone to market for the last 100 years. There could be a "Sonic" SUV or a "UAG", coupe or "Asbury" convertible on a lot somewhere for sale. The possibilities are limitless with branding becoming the driving force.

Another trend in the car business is that several Dealers admit that their real estate ventures are now a more important part of their business planning than their automotive segment. Many dealerships that were built 20 to 50 years ago are now sitting on some very prime real estate. This land is needed for regional and local development. A lot of Dealers are cashing in on the inflated value of their property. This economic reality has forced some Dealers to face the economic reality of franchise consolidation in facilities that they own rather than relocate to a more expensive piece of real estate somewhere else.

Manufacturers are more flexible with facilities planning than they once were. Right now, they are scrambling to maintain a presence in key markets while trying to reduce Dealer count in rural and weak markets. They are not always demanding the monumental facilities that they once did.

There are exceptions, of course, and some markets continue to feel the factory pressure to build, expand or relocate the franchise. Many of those manufacturers are dictating how and when a Dealer will spend his money to build the business. There has always been a trend in facilities planning to have a uniquely identifiable franchise by the look of the building. In contrast, a lot of dealers today are more interested in the cross-functionality of their facility and building their own local brand than a unique factory brand look. The compromise solution seems to be a facility which can address everyone's needs with separate show rooms, repair shops and display lots.

The public's perception is that automobile manufacturers have been slow to make product adjustments for market demand. An example would be the publics' demand for more fuel efficient vehicles. When trucks were king, there was a practical marketing approach that matched customer needs. Remember the market trend to move into minivans? Chrysler jumped right in and led the charge. Ford and GM were a little slow to respond to this trend. Then, in the late 90's the move was from minivans to SUV's, and that happened quickly. The race was on for more cup holders in mini-vans and bigger pay-loads in truck beds. Soon the market was filled with huge vehicles that looked more like school busses and monster trucks.

Manufacturers who were slow to recognize customer needs, chose instead to tell the customer what they wanted. Dealers in the past, have been hung with a variety of odd product offerings that the public just did not want. The factories frequently took an existing vehicle platform and added sheet metal styling to meet some market demand. Sometimes they missed the mark and those vehicles sat on dealer lots for a very long time.

SUV's are a soccer Mom's dream, because she could get everything, including the kids into one vehicle. Trucks too, just kept getting bigger. The cost of gas was cheaper in bygone days than by today's standards. Today gasoline is forecasted to exceed $4.00, up to a possible $7.00 a gallon. The cost of fuel and bad press has made the SUV public enemy number one. Too bad, the need is still there for most Americans but market trends and attitudes continue to change. That is why we have seen the emergence of the Crossover Vehicle. Crossovers are station wagons with all-wheel drive transmissions that can get up and go in any weather and in some cases, still deliver decent gas mileage. Manufacturers are listening to their customers.

Dealers who have more than one franchise know that each of their factory agreements require that they have a separate service department for each of their brands. Manufacturers like to define their brand with a separate a show room and a separate service facility for their customers. In single point dealerships this creates no conflict.

Multi-franchise dealers have built facilities with separate show rooms and service write-up areas. Some of them send all of the vehicles, regardless of brand, back to a single service repair shop. I am told that customers don't seem to notice or that they don't care. One thing is for sure, most customers do want the confidence of knowing that a Chevy factory trained Technician is taking care of their Chevrolet for their repair work. This concept is true for Chevrolet and it is true for all manufactured brands of vehicles.

We know that customers want factory trained Technicians performing their warranty and repair work for their brand of vehicle. So, if you have a single point dealership or several brands represented on your lot, the question remains, what is the best formula for handling quick service maintenance and light repairs in your shop? If you have several name plates on your building, you are probably looking at costly and repetitive duplication of quick service operations in each shop. The alternative is to pay your highly priced "A" Technicians to do the work. Ouch! In order to keep your factory happy as well as your customers, you may need to consider other options. One solution is a separate quick service facility that can service all makes and all models for all quick service and light repair.

Where you choose to perform the repair work in your operation is your business. Your customers will judge your dealership's performance each time they bring a vehicle into your business. Like it or not, we are in the business of pleasing other people in order to make a profit.

CHAPTER 5

THE SERVICE CUSTOMERS EXPERIENCE

Customer Satisfaction Indexes provide a guide as to how well a customer receives what is delivered. CSI is the report card that tells Dealers how they are doing in the marketplace. In this business, it is easy to become focused on moving vehicle volume and loosing track of what customers really want. Even with a CSI report on our desk we become so focused on numbers that we forget the human element.

Dealers sometimes get defensive and take on an "us vs. them" attitude with customers. They blame the factory for tying CSI to incentives and programs. Even with the pressures of working sales volume and factory programs, most dealer principals are really pretty sensitive to customer perception. They want the public to consider their dealership the best place to shop for vehicles. They want to believe that everyone in the dealership is working for the same goals that they are.

Unfortunately, the way things are in most dealerships is not the way the Dealer or the Service Manager really wants them to be. Running the Parts and Service department can be compared to fine tuning a large symphonic orchestra. You need to have all of the parts and pieces work in complementary harmony. There are a lot of sour notes if everyone is not on the same page. One sour note for many Dealers is keeping customers happy so that they will return to the dealership.

The old adage, "no good deed goes unpunished."

Someone in the car business decided to define the customer experience in a dealership as either **completely satisfied** or **unsatisfied**. Nothing in-between seems to matter to those tabulating the measurements. Think about it, no gentleman in his right mind would ever ask his wife if she was completely satisfied, yet this is the standard Dealers are expected to live up to.

Most dealerships do a pretty good job of completely satisfying customers as they come through their doors on a day to day basis. Whole systems have been invented to address how to satisfy customers. In many recommended process, the solutions fall too late, after a problem has already occurred.

A customer situation that I hear frequently from Dealers is where the dealership has performed some service operation for the customer. Something didn't go right, so at some great expense to the dealership management will go out on a limb and over compensates the customer for their experience through goods, service or labor. About 40 days later the customer burns the dealership on the CSI report. It seems like no matter what is done the customer cannot be completely satisfied. A Dealer once told me, "It is hard to get a charging rhino into reverse." He's right!

A Service customer's experience in a new car dealership has a lot to do with the expectations that have been set for them before they get to the Service isle. They have already drawn some conclusions based on what may have happened in the sales delivery process or from a prior service experience. Many customers do not look forward to visiting their Service department. They put that experience right up there with having a root canal.

Customers have one set of expectations and what is delivered is frequently another. Overcoming all of these preconceived notions is a major task for a Service department. Somehow you must win them over to the land of "Complete Satisfaction". But where is the "whoopee zone," the "wow factor," the "I'm totally impressed" feeling that is often missing?

We have all heard that perception is reality. This always irritated me until I read that Einstein once said "perception is the accumulation of all prior knowledge and wisdom, therefore it can be changed." Dealers have the opportunity to change perceptions by changing the customers' experience every time they come through the door. Just be sure to make it a good one.

There is a car Dealer in Brooklyn, NY who offers a free buffet lunch every day. But to really entice his customers, the Dealer and his co-workers break out in song, like in a Broadway play, as a way to entertain his customers and provide an experience unlike any they had ever received in a dealership before. Is this over the top? Perhaps but the customers keep coming back to buy cars and to get their vehicles serviced.

Now a look at the service experience from the customer's point of view:

For arguments sake, we will look at a typical customer experience for a 15,000 mile oil change and a tire rotation. Simple! Huh? To begin with, customers feel like they can get an oil change in 20-30 minutes or less but the reality is far from what is expected.

When an oil change customer drives up to a new car dealership they look for directional signage that takes them to a part of the building that says SERVICE in big letters. Most new car Service departments are set up where a Service isle is either inside or outside the building. A customer may drive up with or with out an appointment. A Service Advisor will meet them and record the customer's primary concern on a Customer Pay Repair Order. In this case an oil and filter change at 15,000 miles.

Customers are often encouraged to make an appointment before they come into a dealership to have their vehicle serviced. Scheduling an appointment has very little to do with scheduling and loading the Technician work load in the shop. Appointments have more to do with the convenience of write-up for the Service Advisors, to spread the write-up process throughout the day. Even with appointments, most dealerships operate on a first come first serve basis and appointments are almost never used for assignment of work in the shop to any particular Technician or work group.

Now, if you are the customer and you make an appointment for 10:00 AM then 10:00 AM is when the customer expects the work to begin. A customer might even show up a little early, thinking that the work will get done faster. Unfortunately, they just wait longer.

Let's take the case of going to a dentist, for comparison purposes. If you go to the dentist for a 10:00 AM appointment, the dental technician is right there to usher you into a chair. In fact, even before you get to the dental office, someone generally calls to confirm that you will actually be in for your scheduled appointment. Some medical doctors are now making their patients sign a form that holds the customer responsible for the cost of a doctor's time if the patient fails to show up for an appointment. These professionals are taking their money making opportunities seriously.

Customers who come into new car dealerships and expect to get their work performed while they wait are referred to in our business as "waiters." Customers come in with the expectation that an oil change should not take too long, so they stick around. Waiters are sometimes instructed to come in for their service appointment by someone in the dealership other than the Service Advisor and told that they would not need an appointment. Other waiters simply cannot afford to be without their vehicles, so they sit and wait.

Customers expect quick service because they can get this kind of service at competing aftermarket service facilities all over town. They can get this service at franchise oil change shops, tire stores and a mom and pop repair shops. So they come into car dealerships and wait, and wait, and wait.

The sad experience for some of these waiters is that the expectation of a 20-30 minute oil change may really take up to 2-3 hours. The unfortunate fact is, that some long waits for vehicles are simply a break-down in a dealerships process follow-through, not the length of time it takes to get an oil change in and out of the shop. It is no wonder, that new vehicle customers dread the experience of going into their new car dealership's Service department for simple maintenance services that can be provided by friendly, convenient and price conscious aftermarket service competitors.

Below are some typical steps for our "waiter" with a 15,000 mile oil change and a tire rotation:

- The customer drives to the Service isle and is greeted by a Service Advisor. With pen in hand the Service Advisor records the customers Vehicle Identification Number (VIN) and note the customer's name. Depending on how many customers there are in the Service isle that morning the customer may get a smile and a cup of coffee but generally all they receive is "What can I do for you?" or "What ch'a got?"

The word "service" on the door implies that work will be performed by one who serves. Look it up in any dictionary. Service is for the help or benefit of the customer. A far better greeting for customers should be; "How may I serve you today?" or "How may I help you today?"…and then <u>smile</u> like you mean it. I don't see many Service Advisors smiling in car dealerships.

- The Service Advisor will then go to the write-up area and type in the Vehicle Identification Number (VIN) into the company's computer. This is done to see if the customers' vehicle comes up on the computer screen. If nothing appears they then type in the customers name and hope for the best. Finally, if that does not work they must ask the customer if they have ever been into this dealership for service before, with this vehicle. If not, this customer is immediately labeled a "visiting owner." The Service Advisor must then go through the process of building a customer file for this visit which, in some dealerships, may take some time.

- Once the customer and the vehicle are identified in the dealerships' computer, the Service Advisor will then ask some open ended questions, such as, "What can I do for you?" or "Can you tell me what's going on with your vehicle?". The Service Advisor then types the customer's reason for the visit. This is called the "concern." In our example, the customer came in for a oil and filter change and a tire rotation repair. A labor operation code is then attached to this concern and it becomes the primary reason the customer came into the dealership. This is called the "primary concern."

- The Service Advisor may or may not run the VIN through a factory data base to check on any outstanding campaigns or recalls. If the vehicle has low mileage or very high mileage some Service Advisors assume that there are no outstanding campaigns on that vehicle and may miss an important opportunity for taking care of the customer and earning additional service revenue for the shop.

- The Service Advisor may or may not present a pre-printed menu of maintenance items that are recommended at various mileage intervals for the vehicle.

- The Service Advisor may or may not visually inspect the customer's tires, windshield wiper blades and general condition of the vehicle. The Service Advisor should look for dents and dings to record on the repair order to avoid being claimed by the customer later. Time may be spent with a cursory look over the vehicle for the Vehicle Inspection Report that many manufacturers require. This step is often overlooked on a 15,000 mile vehicle.

- If the customer should have any additional repair requests, they are recorded as second or third concerns on the repair order. The repair order is printed for the Technicians as a "work order." If the customer is a waiter, most dealerships identify the repair order with a stamp or some method to let the shop know that a customer is waiting on this vehicle. **Lexus dealerships have a practice of switching-on the emergency lights to keep everyone in the shop aware that this vehicle has a waiting owner in the customer lounge.**

- The "waiter" customer is directed to a customer waiting area. Customer's expectations are not set because they are typically not told when the work may be completed.

- The vehicle is removed from the Service isle by a Porter, Technician or the Service Advisor to a Service parking slot behind the shop. This is the stage where the customer sees their vehicle disappear out of the Service isle door and they get that "sinking feeling" that they may never see their vehicle again.

- The oil change Technician will look for and discover the vehicle in the Service lot. The vehicle will be pulled onto a Service lift rack and the oil change process begun. **Not all oil change Technicians are empowered to look for anything other than an oil filter**. The enterprising ones will pull the air filter, inspect the tires and check all of the fluid levels.

- Most dealerships offer a standard lube, oil and filter service affectionately referred to in the business as an LOF. Without any further instruction, an OF is generally all the customer gets. The vehicle will receive no top off of fluids, no battery inspection, no wiper blade inspection, no tire air pressure inspection or fuel filter inspection and in most cases, not even a lube from the LOF. The customer asked for an oil change and a tire rotation so the dealership assumes, by-golly that is what they will get.

- Most new car manufacturers encouraged their Dealers to perform vehicle inspections providing a preprinted form for the dealership to use, at a charge of course. The top copy on these forms is intended to go to the customer, the second copy is to be attached to the work order and the last copy is to go into a follow-up file for declined services so the dealership can call these customers later for declined repairs. The last copy is rarely used for the purpose for which it was intended.

While performing 100 Customer Pay repair order studies in car dealerships all over this great land, I have discovered 3 copy inspection reports that were completed and stapled to the repair order accounting copy or to the service history file copy. These forms may cost the Dealer up to 75¢ each. In other words, the customer never saw the inspection report. Sometimes Employees do this thinking they are in compliance with a manufacturer inspection requirement. The customer was never able to gain the confidence that someone is looking after their best interests. Yet dealership personnel keep squandering the dealer's net profit for nothing.

On further inspection of these reports, the inspections were often hit and miss. Technicians would simply put a line through all of the boxes or just did not bother to check them at all. This behavior is often justified by Service Advisors for lower or very high mileage vehicles, but keep in mind that the dealer has paid for each form.

Technicians tell me that when they do a thorough inspection and note the needed repairs, the Service Advisors often do not sell the work. They loose confidence and the inspection process breaks down. Most shops have one or two guys who will just not get with the inspection program. It is up to management to make the system work.

- Once an Oil Change has been completed, the Technician may perform the tire rotation. The oil change Technician may not actually perform the tire rotation that our customer requested. This labor may be the responsibility of another Technician who does this work in a specialized service bay. Hopefully, the rotation is not overlooked.
- Unfortunately, tires on vehicles are quickly rotated without a thorough inspection. With out that inspection we are simply sending these customers on their way with potential safety issues. Imagine; nuts, bolts screws, nails, and more in customer tires or damaged rims as they drive out of the dealership.

  Who is this customer going to blame when something happens to their vehicle? What happens when they have a flat tire that results in an accident and your dealership is the last place they had service work performed? Tilt! You had better make sure that your lawyer's retainer is up to date or that a through inspection is completed.

- The "Cause" and "Correction" sections of the repair order should be completed by the Technician on every work order. It is amazing how many are left blank. I often recommend that oil Technicians clock on and off tickets just like a flat rate Technician, even if they are hourly. Tracking service work through your shop is critical even with hourly employees.
- The Technician will pull the vehicle out of the oil bay and park it again in the service lot. Some shops have a service hat or tag to identify the vehicle. From this point, the process varies from

dealership to dealership. The oil Technician may walk the work order to the Service Advisor so they can "close" the ticket. Some systems are automated and rely on the Service Advisor to check a "tickler" file periodically to see if the work has been completed by the Technician.

- The Service Advisor will "close" the ticket and walk the paper work and the keys to the cashier. Sometimes the work order and keys are taken directly to the cashier by the Technician. The Cashier will hang on to the keys and close the ticket and print a receipt when the customer goes to the Cashier's area with payment.

- How the customer is informed that their vehicle is ready varies wildly. The responsibility for this act could fall on the Service Advisor, smoke signals or even a loud speaker system informing a customer that they need to go to the Cashier's area.

- Customers will often review the bill and ask the cashier what they know about the service that was performed. After a blank stare from the Cashier he/she will call, over the loud speaker, for someone from Service department to come to the Cashier's area. In some cases, when the customer is not satisfied with the bill, they are sent back into the Service department to search for the Service Advisor to address their concerns on their own.

- The Cashier will then notify a Porter or someone in Service department to find the customers car and bring it around to the Service isle. This simple task can often take some time because no one may be aware as to where the oil change Technician may have left the vehicle or even worse, where the vehicle's keys are.

- Finally, the customer may or may not be thanked for their business. A Service Advisor may, or may not, schedule a follow-up maintenance visit and the customer will drive away thinking "Why did I spend all of that time here just for an oil change?"

These steps are not common to all dealerships and probably not in your business. The process flow, however, is typical of many Service departments.

This is what happens with a simple oil change and tire rotation. When you add an additional repair to the work order the steps become far more complex. A customer with a Customer Pay drivability concern (a repair that involves the performance of the engine or transmission), for example, could be in for a very long wait. Just a second repair concern could cost the customer a great deal of wait time. The vehicle may get recycled through the Service department several times for multiple repairs by specialized Technicians. In my experience, I have watched customers grow old in dealership waiting lounges.

CHAPTER 6

HOW SERVICE DEPARTMENTS OPERATE

Production Systems:

The reason to look at production systems is that you really need to get a handle on how work is managed and moves through your shop before you make any serious changes.

There are a number of ways to organize workload in a service shop. Your dealership is using some form of production system to move work through the shop. Many Dealers have inherited the production system they are currently using while others have instituted programs based on consulting advice. The choice is yours to make depending on what the dynamics of your particular shop are but it is wise to make an informed decision based on as much information as you can gather.

Some Dealers are blessed with outstanding employees. They have real leaders in their organization that know how to capitalize on opportunities as they are presented. Others languish with low producing Technicians who barely post 35 hours a week. It seems kind of strange to have employees who show up to work in a flat rate shop and yet they can barely manage to post 40 hours a week.

You only have an inventory of so many bays in your shop. Each bay is worth so many hours that can be billed. Therefore, you have an inventory of potential hours at the beginning of each and every day to sell in each service bay. Your goal should be to maximize this opportunity.

Service bays are useless unless you have Technicians to work in them. If you have a Technician who shows up to work for a 40 hour week and he produces 40 billable hours of work he is 100% productive. This is what you want 100% of the time, right? I know what you are thinking, "Hell no, I want a Technician showing up 40 hours a week and billing 80 hours." This is a reasonable leap of faith but stay with me.

Therefore, if you have10 bays with 10 lifts, you have an inventory of 80 hours to sell for the day. If you're effective labor rate is $75.00 per hour and if 10 Technicians are 100% productive then you should be selling $6,000 per day or $600 per bay per day.

Simple, huh?

The reality is, many of you have 10 bays with 5 Technicians who are about 70% proficient. So you actually sell only 56 of the 80 potential hours at $57.00 (effective labor rate) for $3192 per day or $319 per bay per day. You managed to get 280 hours of Technician time of the 400 in inventory.

Many dealerships, on the average, are only selling about 2-3 hours per bay per day and their Technicians are only about 70% productive. That means the average dealership is only earning about $157 per bay per day. That is leaving a lot of money on the table.

Why is this number so low? There are as many reasons as there are Service Managers to explain the difference.

The number one reason is that Dealers have bought into the idea that a Technician needs two Service bays and in some cases even more. If you have an idle bay with a vehicle waiting for parts on a lift, how much money are you making during the wait?

In the eastern part of the country where real estate is high and space in shops is scarce, Technicians get only one bay. They may have to push a vehicle out of the way to make room for another while they wait on parts. If any given Technician owned his own shop, he would certainly make room for another vehicle while he waited on parts. New car Technicians have the luxury of your business to warehouse vehicles while they wait on parts.

Where does the time go?

In some smaller shops, Technicians are required to do other duties besides turning wrenches. Time not spent on a service job will erode into their productive time. Other Technicians are slow but very thorough. What these guys lack in productivity they will make up for in fewer come-backs and higher customer satisfaction, even at the sacrifice of their own paychecks. Yet there are some techs are just not skilled enough to do the work that is assigned to them and they muddle through jobs all day long.

Finally, some Technicians are just lazy and inefficient. Can these technicians be culled from the workforce? Do your Technicians clock off a repair ticket while they wait for parts? If not, this will make a difference in production as well.

Some Dealers will retain a poor performing employee because they are factory certified to do warranty work. You have made the choices about who works in your shop. A service performance analysis and periodic employee performance reviews will provide you with answers about how your Technicians are working for you. Finally, you have to ask yourself, how many Technicians in any given shop really need two Service bays to themselves?

Technicians forget who they work for sometimes. They will push-back claiming that they can always make more money working for their brother-in-laws independent shop. I heard one trainer say "Tell them goodbye! That is why tool chests have wheels on them." Reality suggests that you do not have enough techs now and few shops can ill afford to simply tell people to go.

Technicians who claim they can make more money in an independent shop have overlooked a few things. There is the initial capital investment, working capital, credit lines to buy parts, tools and supplies, a marketing plan to generate new business, very long hours, no vacations to go deer hunting, no cash reserve to cover the overhead, no benefits like health insurance and sick pay to think of. In today's world, it really does not take much to become another statistic on the failed business list. Technicians are at dealerships for a reason. For them going to work at a new car Dealer is like moving into the major-leagues. There is a certain status associated with working at a new car dealership. Keep in mind that if you have a great Technician and they are doing a great job you should treat them very well. If you have a dud, cull the heard.

Review your personnel quarterly and make adjustments. Choose your people carefully and feel free to move people around into other positions in the dealership. This move can expand employee horizons and encourage poor performers to move along if they don't like the work.

What are Production Systems?

Production systems are just ways to identify the process steps followed to move work through a repair shop efficiently. Your Service department's job is to produce billable hours on repair orders. You have an investment into a building that has a finite number of Service bays. Each bay is an opportunity to make money. Every day that you get up and come to work, your shop has an inventory of just so many hours to sell for each service stall. What more can you do to improve your shop?

Dealers try to make more money in the shop by changing how the work flows through the shop. Changing a production system can often help to improve customer satisfaction and in some cases will improve Technician productivity.

A Few Production Methods:

Below is a description of a few production methods of moving work through the shop. Most of them are designed to keep Technicians busy. Some of them are for the benefit of a Service Advisor. All of these methods are in use in car dealership Service departments today:

- The Service Manager dispatches work directly to Technicians. Small shops will frequently use this method.
- Service Advisor puts work orders in a rack and Technicians pick and choose what work they want to do. Surprisingly this was the main system employed for many years by most dealerships before computers.
- Service Advisors hand work orders or electronically post them to a dispatcher who manually hands the work order to Technicians on a first-come-first-served basis. This is a job for a person who likes a lot of control and is a bottleneck creating a lot of inefficiency. Favoritism and cronyism creep into this method. Most dealerships favor this system.
- Service Advisors hand work orders to a dispatcher who will provide work to Technicians by a shop specialization for a primary repair

item. Once that job is completed the work is again re-dispatched to another specialized Technician. This system is familiar to the medical profession.

- Service Advisors dispatch directly to any Technician in a specialized shop. This means the Service Advisor will need to re-dispatch to another Technician for each concern on a multiple repair ticket unless the assigned Technician is empowered to "clean the ticket" or finish all the work on the repair order.

- Service Advisors dispatch work to any Technician in a cross functional shop where any Technician may work on a ticket, regardless of Technician pay structure or skill level. I call this the quid pro quo system. I have witnessed Service Advisors walking around the shop begging Technicians to take a particular job.

- Service Advisors will hand work orders to a Service Manager who will then hand work to Technicians. When this happens there has been a breakdown in moving work through the shop. The Service Manager takes control with the attitude, "if you want it done right, you must do it yourself."

- Service Advisors dispatch work to Technicians supervised by a shop whip or Foreman, who decides which Technicians will actually perform the work. This is called the "Little Tyrant" or "Dictator" system.

- Service Advisors dispatch to Technicians with the use of an electronic dispatch system. This system has been faulted because skill levels are not always maintained in the DMS system. Some managers claim that Technicians can dodge jobs and override the work dispatched to them. There are controls and passwords that can prevent this from happening but the system upkeep is tiresome.

- Service Advisor Team - work is dispatched by a Service Advisor to a team of Technicians with use of an electronic dispatch system, no favorites. A team leader may make the final decision as to who performs the work.

- Service Advisor Team - where Service Advisors dispatch work orders directly to a team leader who then distributes work to the Technicians on his team. The team is paid on group or team production rather than individual flat rate. This is sometimes called a true team system. I have heard some people call it socialism.

- Service Advisor Team - where Service Advisors dispatch work orders to individual members of their assigned team. This is frequently called a Lateral Support Group. This system is favored by many shops. Unfortunately, teams frequently have an uneven Technician certification and skill level between them. Customers do not remember if they are on a red or blue team. If they are color blind, well, who knows where they might wind up? In a Service Advisor Team, the advisors dispatch directly to the Oil/Lube/tire person or team. The work order comes back after the oil change is completed then the ticket is re-dispatched to another Technician for a primary concern. Sometimes this is done in reverse order depending on shop load.

- Some Service isles have an oil change Service Advisor who will hand work orders to the lube rack Technician. Work orders are returned and handed to another Service Advisor who will re-dispatch the primary concern to a different Technician.
- Service Advisors dispatch to a maintenance team with a flat rate Technician. They will perform a variety of quick services and tire work and complete all inspections. If there is a primary concern item beyond maintenance the work order is returned and the work is then re-dispatched to a line Technician with the proper skill level. This just makes too much sense and hardly anyone does it.

All of these systems have several bottlenecks. Shop work can get bogged down and delayed in any process step, especially when there is more than one line item on the repair ticket. Workflow problems creep up if an employee fails to show for work. Most dealerships have no back-up plans for employees who are missing in action. Cross-training is almost unheard of. If you only get one thing out of this book, take the time to cross-train your employees.

The main reason for delays during production, dispatch and delivery of the vehicle to the customer, is frequently the simple oil change and tire rotation on a multiple line repair ticket. If a customer has an oil change, a tire rotation and a "check and advise" on a window regulator, the vehicle could get tied up for a couple of days.

No matter what production system a Dealer uses there are always opportunities to change and improve. Most Dealers would rather have all of their teeth pulled than walk out into the shop and tell the Technicians that everything has just changed. Dealers need to change what they are doing, however, if they want to improve production in their repair shops. So how do they do it?

A positive way for any dealership to change is to move the inspections of oil changes, tire work and light repair from the cumbersome main shop and segment this work it into a separate department. Segmenting will allow your line Technicians the opportunity to focus on work that is more suited to their skill level. They may squawk about loosing gravy work but you can compromise. If they find a brake job on their assigned repair order then they should be able to "clean the ticket" and book the time. They won't loose any more time than they are loosing now and they probably won't find any more additional repair work to sell than they do now.

Another consideration for every shop is to use a grid pricing program for selling customer service work. If you are already on one, review it and become more aggressive in its use. In most cases, there are more exceptions than reasons for employees to stick to a grid. This just means that employees do not buying in to your vision of dealership management. They may even feel that your grid system is broken. Every time the grid is overridden the Dealer has just lost money. You can review this by looking at your service invoicing exception report. Take a look at the dollars and number of overrides in your system. Check it monthly.

Lower your overall cost of sale by lowering your average Technician pay in the shop with Technicians who are paid less. Hire more B and C Technicians. Use them as helpers to certified techs. Gain some production efficiencies and put a lift in every bay. Go down the street and hire the guys that the light repair shops are using. Make sure you have the right guy running your shop.

Service Managers:

A Service Manager is the multi-functional, multi-tasking Swiss army knife of the dealership. They come in all sizes, shapes, personalities and skill levels. Some can be classed as good at what they do and some are no better than caretakers who let the Technicians run the shop. They are all there to help the Dealer make money. The responsibilities of a new car dealership Service Manager go beyond keeping labor grosses high. Departmental labor gross is how we pay them though. Think of everything that is asked of them and then look at where the reward system is based.

If you write a job description for the position of Service Manager where would you begin? By the way, you should write a job description for every position in the dealership. Then ask every employee to do the same. Make a comparison and see what the results are. You will be surprised. They are doing all kinds of things you did not know they are doing. More importantly, they are probably not doing the things that you think they should be doing. This is a great exercise.

Do you just assume that if a Service Manager has worked in a Service department somewhere that they would have all of the skills necessary to run and manage your Service department? Service Managers are frequently promoted to their position simply because of the convenience of being there, on site, when someone left. Promotion was the easy and economical thing to do at the time. But what are the real job skills for handling the position?

First of all, no two dealerships are alike. Likewise, each Service department needs are as different as their cliental. Should a Service Manager be a skilled technical person or should they be good with people? The skills and characteristics that we look for in people are called attributes. Below are a few attributes to consider when hiring a Service Manager.

- Service Managers need to **communicate** effectively with owners and upper management.
- Service Managers need to **communicate** effectively, with-out conflict, with Managers in other departments; like the Parts Department, Body Shop, Used Vehicles and New Car Sales and the Administrative Office.
- Service Managers need to **communicate** effectively with customers of the dealership.
- Service Managers need to **communicate** effectively with Technicians. They need to understand the skill level and personality of each Technician so that a production goal of 100% or greater can be achieved. A Service Manager must be a leader and a coach.

- Service Managers need to **communicate** effectively with Service Advisors so that they thoroughly and completely understand their rolls and tasks to sell more hours per ticket.
- Service Managers need to have a marketing plan and know how to execute it effectively.
- Service Managers need to establish an accountability system for all service employees.
- Service Managers need to work with Cashiers and office staff and understand the paperwork flow.
- Service Managers need to understand the warranty requirements for manufacturers represented by the dealerships franchises. They are the gatekeeper to keep the Dealer out of "warranty jail."
- Service Managers need to have a complete understanding of the service software being used by the dealership.
- Service Managers need to be able to **communicate** effectively and be a diplomat with the factory representatives.
- Service Managers need to know how to **communicate** effectively with vendors and understand how to leverage this resource to the dealerships advantage.
- Service Managers need to have a complete understanding of the controllable expenses of the Service department and how to manage them effectively. Only Service Managers who can see their page of the financial statement can be effective at expense control.
- Service Managers need to understand the concept of net profit or how the Dealer gets paid.

Everything on this list is a tall order for any one person to fill. You want the person who in grade school, always got high marks in the "works and plays well with others" category.

In case you didn't notice, communication should be the key factor in seeking a Service Manager candidate. Keep in mind that communication needs to flow both up and down in your dealership. The information chain needs to work from the Technician to the owner and back again. The Service Manager is the conduit for these messages.

How many people can a manager effectively manage? At Ford Motor Co. we used to say a manager should have no more than 6 direct reports. Most

Service Managers are in charge of many more than that. If so, how effective are they? Harvard Business studies indicate that managers with too many direct reports tend to spend all of their time putting out fires instead of performing the management duties that they are hired to do. These managers seem to do everything themselves rather than delegate, which means they are hard to be held accountable. It is real easy for an over-tasked manager to get burned-out and non productive. Without hiring more people, departments can be re-structured with delegated job duties to assist the Service Manager. You have to be smarter than the problem.

Over tasked Service Managers sometimes loose control of the shop to Technicians. Service Managers who were once Technicians have sympathy for how things are done out in the shop and they do not want to rock the boat with temperamental employees. Too often, Technicians are able to take advantage. Many will try to perform "outside work" in dealership stalls, after hours. Whose dollars should those be? Whose parts are they using? Will an effective Service Manager be on top of this activity?

Are Service Managers a reflection of their pay plans? Service Managers are generally paid a percentage of departmental gross on labor hours billed and they are held accountable for expenses. Technicians are generally paid on labor operations for flat rate hours on tickets. It is the Service Managers job to keep the work moving through the shop to see that tickets get closed. On the other hand, Technicians get paid, in many cases, even if a ticket is not yet closed from a daily time and job ticket. This little difference contributes to unapplied time. A Service Manager is paid on the results of the prior month's business. They are so busy putting out fires that they may not focus on expense.

Who are you going to hire?

According to the author, Dave Anderson of *Up Your Business*, you should be "slow to hire and quick to fire." Most Dealers view their employees as family members. In some rural communities, employees may actually be family members or neighbors, making hiring and firing decisions even tougher. Dealers are reluctant to fire because they are not sure that they can recruit the kind of people they want, for what they want to pay them. They just keep the same poor performers around and get the same results.

Dealers are afraid to hire from another town or community, in case things do not work out. Dealers in smaller communities tell me, that they just do not want to be financially responsible for bringing someone in from the outside. Change is just too risky for these Dealers.

If you want to move to the next level, you will need to research and look hard for the people you want in your business. Obtaining the right people is labor intensive but rewarding. Hire a head hunter, if necessary. Review many resumes and thoroughly check the information on the applications that have been submitted to you. Don't make a quick and easy choice. Set up a competitive pay plan that will compensate your employees for performance goals that you establish.

When I coached youth soccer I had some pretty outstanding teams. I would like to think that the team's success was inspired coaching but to be honest, the difference from one season to the next depended entirely on the players that I was able to get and how skilled they were when I got them. If I found a player with some natural talent and was I able to bring out the best in that player my team was that much stronger. The difference in a winning season and a loosing season was the difference in the players that had been assigned to me. Your business is no different.

The difference in a profitable Service department and one that is in a loss position, frequently, is the people you have in your department. Be prepared to make changes to get the best results. If you do not feel comfortable firing people then change the job responsibilities and duties of the people you want out. Move a few people around to make your dealership stronger. The employee may get the message and become more productive or simply leave the dealership on their own. The strength of your dealerships Service department is a reflection of the strength of your character as a Dealer.

Service Department Management – What your Customers See.

The one thing that scares customers to death is the dreaded "Posted Labor Rate" and "Diagnostic Charge" hanging on car dealership walls. This is what the dealership declares that they charge for all Customer Pay work. Customers see that posted labor rate and they think, "No one should make that much money." Customers see this and they cannot flee fast enough. The "One Hour" diagnostic charge to look at a concern is intimidating. In some shops the diagnostic charge is not even applied to the repair. Plumbers and Electricians charge "look at fees" and it annoys the heck out of me.

No one wants to work for free. The one hour diagnostic fee is charged to the customer no matter how much time was spent figuring out what the concern actually is. Customers find this irritating because they know your Technician didn't spend a whole hour looking at their vehicle. The simple answer is to graduate the diagnostic fee to the type of repair and apply the fee to the actual repair. Do not tell the customer that you are charging an hour of posted labor rate to them, this will only turn ugly.

Posted labor rates or the Customer Pay Door Rate is what you would really like to earn on each hour of labor sold in your shop. The reality is, that many of you are earning between 55-75% of that posted labor rate. What you actually earn on each hour of labor sold is your Effective Labor Rate.

When your effective labor rate is off by 15% or more, you are not getting the most out of your shop. Your Technician productivity could be down. Your Service Advisors may be making adjustments in pricing to meet the competition. Getting business is good, even if you have to buy it, I guess, but if you are constantly making changes on your repair orders then something is broke. The crime comes when every once in awhile, you have that unsuspecting customer who comes through the door and they pay full mark-up on labor and parts while the last 10 people in front of them got a discount special. Goals should be obtainable. Keep your posted labor rate (door rate) and your effective labor rate with-in 90% of each other. Don't actually post the labor rate on the door.

Your after-market competition has a posted labor rate too. In most cases their effective labor rate is much closer to their posted labor rate, which is lower than yours. Well, they have a lower overhead expense and use aftermarket parts and their cost of labor is lower and so on.

What your competition does is out of your control, you cannot change it. What you can control is your cost of sale (yes, even in a union shop), your Technician productivity, service bay productivity, hours per repair order, parts per repair order, expenses and effective labor rate.

CHAPTER 7

FINDING TECHNICIANS

Finding Technicians is such a great challenge for many Dealers that I decided to dedicate a chapter to the subject. Finding Technicians is not the problem, I am told. Finding good reliable certified Technicians is the issue. There are many reasons why certified Technicians are not immediately available but there are a lot of good talented and reliable Technicians out there, you just have to know where to look.

The warranty landscape is changing. Declining warranty is a reality. Many dealerships are seeing up to 30% less in warranty labor under the prior year. A few dealerships are showing an increase in warranty but by and large the trend is less and less. Certified Technicians are hired at a premium because the automobile manufacturers demand that a trained certified Technician perform warranty work.

Warranty repair work is changing along with many labor operations that require replacement of components rather than repairing components and replacing parts. Warranty work really falls into three categories; component replacement, analyze and repair and factory customer notifications and recalls.

Factories are concerned about warranty expense. They require that a Technician be certified in a skill level so that a repair job can be completed in a specified amount of time to keep warranty expense down.

Does all warranty work need to have Master Certified Technician or are there some warranty labor operations that do not require higher levels of certification for a particular repair job? This concept opens the door to B-level Technicians assisting and performing heavier repair work along side certified "A" Technicians. If you can use "B" techs for some of your diesel and heavy work that you have been saving for certified Technicians, then you should be able to move work through the shop a little faster at a lower cost of labor. You are also providing an on the job training program for your Technicians which can become an incentive for them to achieve certification as well. In order to separate this work load, your Service Manager/Advisor must be very aware of the factory requirements on any warranty repair.

How do you encourage that high-end Master Certified Technician who is turning 80 hours a week to do more analytical work and problem solving? Why would you want to change anything if they are turning 80 hours a week? The answer to both questions is simple. Quality control is important. You need to have several Technicians in your shop turning more hours and they need to be more productive while making fewer mistakes. You need to have complicated problems solved by the best talent in your shop with out a come-back.

The real question is why would the Technician want to do more analytical work if he is making that much money? Somewhere, you and your Technicians are going to have a meeting of the minds on what is best for them and what is best for the dealership. You may have to choose a different pay structure for this type of Technician, in order to get the entire shops production up. Performing these reviews is where your leaders emerge.

Dealerships are running out of Technicians. I am told by Dealers and Service Managers from coast to coast that they cannot find Technicians. Yet there seem to be more and more after market service facilities opening up every day. The light repair facilities down the road are offering repairs up to 3 hours in most cases. They have ASE certified Technicians who perform the more difficult tasks and they use assistants help to turn the work.

The point is you cannot afford to pay your highest paid Technicians to perform oil changes and tire rotations. You need to keep these Technicians busy doing repair work. If you do dispatch an oil change to one of them, they rarely find and sell any additional work on that ticket. They just do not seem hungry enough. Dealers need a better answer.

Top Technicians will have low end work fed to them by Service Advisors in an effort to keep them busy. This is really more of a problem in how your Service Advisors view the work load for the day and how they write up the work. The science of job dispatching by an advisor is frequently second guessing how quickly certain Technicians will complete any given job. An end result of this behavior is the shop is short of work in the afternoon. Service Advisors sometimes undersell work in the shop trying to keep work flow going in an effort to prevent carry-overs. When the techs are suddenly out of work in the afternoon a Service Advisor will send just about anything that comes through the door to the lead Technicians just to feed them work. This costs Service department's money.

Some Service departments plan their work around carry-overs. They want a backlog of work to kick off each day. This takes the pressure off of up-selling in the Service isle. Some Service Advisors will schedule write-ups in the afternoon so that they have an inventory of tickets for the morning. They really have to keep an eye on the traffic flow to make this system work. I have seen some shops so log-jammed that they have given service loaner vehicles to customers just for an oil change. What happens to the waiters in this system? When chaos is king, irrational decisions can trump reason.

How can employees be motivated to do more?

People generally do what they get paid to do, no more or no less. If you want to improve your business you are going to have to think the way your employees think. If your expectations are to have more net profit and happier customers who will buy more vehicles from you then you will have to take a look at how you compensate your employees and make some adjustments along those lines.

If you are looking to make significant changes in your dealership, you cannot just walk in one day show them a cartoon movie about rats moving cheese around and make an announcement that you are turning their world upside down. Ideally, you should work through a process of guided discovery with employee focus groups and develop a consensus before making radical changes. Employees need to feel a sense of empowerment, like the changes are their program. Ownership of a process is critical. The employees will not only look forward to the changes they will lead the charge.

Studies have been performed over and over again and the results are always the same. People look forward to going to work when they have a degree of control over their work load and they can feel a sense of accomplishment. Everyone wants to know that their energy is making some kind of a difference. No one likes the idea of meaningless work in a dead-end job. Drudgery will result in poor moral and lower performance. You, the leader, can change this paradigm.

The mantras for the last 30 or even 40 years seems to be the same; "You break-em we fix-em." "First-come-first-served!" "Warranty feeds the shop." "Let's not sell the customers anything that they do not need." "We don't want to oversell our customers." These are great maxims of a by-gone era. As it turns out, pay plans that stress performance determine how your business functions not old maxims.

Let's take a look at how some car dealership positions are paid. Oil change guys are paid by the hour and are told to turn as many vehicles as they can.

Porters are paid by the hour. Cashiers are paid an hourly wage. Technicians are paid an hourly wage based on hours turned (surprisingly, not always on hours billed). Service Advisors are paid on labor hours billed (many receive no parts compensation and often nothing for writing up warranty). Warranty clerks are generally hourly people who get some kind of a spiff for a good ratio of claims paid to claims submitted (not how much was paid or monitoring claim activity to help keep the Dealer free of audits). Service Managers are paid for the most part on departmental labor gross. All of these people are expected to perform tasks that go beyond the definition of how they get paid. The Dealer will get paid after everyone else has been paid and they are paid on net profit.

At times, everybody in the Service department seems to be moving in a different direction. Some dealerships blow through oil changes with no inspections. Technicians play a game called beat the clock and will even miss installing parts on jobs when they are in a hurry. Porters will loose keys, loose cars and frequently miss work. There are Service Advisors who will hand out service loaners to anyone who asks and then fail to get the customer back into the shop. Through all of this chaos vehicles are serviced and customers show up each day, thank God. Eventually, in the end, it will be the Service Manager, who will put out fires and make order out of the mess, with dead aim focus on gross. That leaves the Dealer each month asking about expense control, customer satisfaction, customer retention, higher Technician productivity, higher effective labor rates and all of the things that will result in better relations between the Sales and Service departments.

How do you get your people on your program? A compensation review will help you and your employee's lazar beam on what you are trying to accomplish. In the end, you may need to take a second look at your entire service operation and decide how you can make several decisive changes.

One key change that can re-structure the shop for greater efficiency and to help you lower your cost of labor, is to move the inefficient oil, tire and light repair business out of the main shop and segment it into a separate operation in your dealership. Many shops experience times of the day when they are busier than others. Frequently the log jam is made worse by the flow of oil changes and tire rotations through a shop. The techs like the gravy work but they don't like changing and rotating tires. They are not going to take the time to inspect the air filter, fuel filter or wiper blades. Very few Technicians will make the time to take the air filter out of the vehicle and walk it up to the customer to show them that it is time to change the filter.

Your employee's pay structure and production methods will translate in to higher customer satisfaction and higher net profits if you re-engineer how you pay them around what your expectations for performance are.

CHAPTER 8

BUILDING CUSTOMER LOYALTY

Customer loyalty is not easily obtained. You want people who return again and again for the goods and services that you offer. With repair shop service, customers defect to the aftermarket for simple reasons. I think we can all agree, that when a vehicle is under warranty, customers will return for warranty repair work. When it comes to maintenance they tend to shop around. After a vehicle is out of warranty, all bets are off. People are going to look for the lowest cost service provider.

Your customer will go down the road for something simple, such as a brother in laws recommendation. Word of mouth and location are the best form of advertising for these repair operations. Customers do not return to the selling Dealer because they feel that no one listens to them or that they were not treated well during the last service visit. What ever the reasons are, your customers are leaving in droves.

You can measure what your customers are doing, a couple of ways. First, measure your dealerships' year over year customer pay tickets. Are your numbers up, down or about the same? Then drive to the aftermarket franchises in your community. Do you see any of your dealership's brand of vehicle in the lot waiting for service?

As a new car Dealer, you have a big advantage over the aftermarket competition. Aftermarkets are in business based on their ability to constantly conquest your customers and take them away. Your job is to keep them. If you continue to give your customers the same service experience they have always received, you will continue to get the same results. In order to grow your business you will need to look at other opportunities.

There is no secret, that import Dealers do a better job of retaining customers than domestic Dealers. This owner loyalty is fostered from day one in an import store and the loyalty is ingrained into the culture of those franchises. Customers have a perception of higher quality and fewer repairs on import vehicles than on domestic brands. The facts do not always support these perceptions but customers who buy import vehicles do maintain their vehicle better than domestic buyers because they believe maintenance increases the value of their vehicle over time. Imports do a better job of retaining their customers for service and when they do that, they have a better shot at selling more new vehicles.

In today's market, all new vehicle dealership operators must have the ability to service and maintain any make or model of vehicle that comes through their service doors. If you are trying to grow your new car business, you will need to conquer and sell more car buyers who are not currently driving your dealership's nameplate. Your competition for vehicle sales is not the other Dealer with the same nameplate down the road; it is the other brand who is converting your customers to their nameplate. One way to keep your customers loyal is to offer maintenance services to all makes and models in your shop. The independent aftermarket service facility down the street panders to every make and model in the market, including yours, so why not you?

The place to start is your Used Car department. Every used car lot will sell more than one make or model. Retaining these customers is a key way to grow your service maintenance business. Your task is to convince the customer that even though you do not have that name plate above your door, you are just as good at maintenance and repairs as the guy down the road. Most new car Dealers do a very poor job of introducing used car customers to their service operations. Remember the dealer who didn't want to see his used vehicle customers again? Are processes in your dealership working to retain the used car customer?

When I approach this subject with Dealers they generally tell me that "my Technicians only work on my brand of vehicle and they reject any work that is not part of their certification." I need to remind them that we are talking about maintenance and light repairs, for the most part, performed by a "B" or "C" level Technician, not a master Technician. Finally, many of the Dealer's Technicians are performing all kinds of work on the side, at home. They work on any make or model of vehicle for their neighbors and friends and maybe even some of your customers.

The road to customer loyalty is for you to take good care of all of your customers all of the time, regardless of the brand they are driving at that moment. Your customers have at least one more car at home, or more. You can win this customer and they will think of you when it comes to buying their next vehicle. Regardless of the brand serviced this repair work all adds gross profit to your business.

How friendly is your Service isle to non-brand customers? Service isles have become advertising tools for manufacturers and a Dealer's first duty is to promote the nameplate on his building. If you segment your quick service operations out of your service isle into a separate write-up area or facility you will have a much friendlier environment for any brand of vehicle.

CHAPTER 9

QUICK SERVICE MODELS

As a car Dealer, where do you begin if you want to take on the aftermarket providers in your community? When I visit car Dealers, I suggest that we get into their vehicle, drive down the road and visit the competition. You need to take a hard look at what they are doing. Competition is everyone else who sells service to your customers. Don't just drive by, go in and talk with the personnel in the aftermarket store, in person. Have your family do some mystery shopping at some of these places. Get prices, gather intelligence on how these businesses operate and take time to interview their employees. I think you will be surprised.

I have never had a problem interviewing people in aftermarket stores. The employees are frequently ready to tell you anything you want to know. Just be candid and up front with them and tell them that you are performing a survey. You might even find a potential employee or two in your quest for more information.

I have summarized how some of the aftermarket franchises do business. Please understand that not all franchise all do business the same way. I have interviewed employees in each of these operations. Most of these operators are good at what they do and just like new car Dealers, some are better than others. They do things that customers want. That is why they can take your customers away.

The Jiffy Lube Experience:

Jiffy Lube and other quick lube franchises like them are very successful for many reasons. Selling oil at a discount price is not one of them. I recently visited a Jiffy Lube and the Manager said, "On a busy day, they would have 12-14 people working to cover the 3 bays." "My 10w30 oil change and air filter cost $48.00."

I went in to get an oil change at Jiffy Lube. They did an excellent job of trying to up sell me. I was shown on screen visual aids of oil menus, and recommended services for the mileage on my vehicle. They escorted me to my vehicle and pointed out the belts and fluid levels. They let me know what condition that my fuel filter and battery were in. They up sold the air filter to me because they took out my old one and compared it to a new one out of the box. "Which do you want me to put back into your vehicle, Mr. Emmett?" I took the clean new one.

Below are several points to look for in a Jiffy Lube:

- Jiffy Lube stores are often found in convenient locations, with-in 3-10 miles of their customer base.
- Quick Lube stores often sit on very expensive real estate. They have a business model that spreads the initial investment over 10 or more years, not one year.
- Convenience: Jiffy Lube stores have extended hours of operation to allow people to come in before work and after work to get their oil changed. Many are open on Saturday and some even on Sunday.

- A lot of oil lube facilities advertise 10 minute oil changes. The actual oil change, indeed, only takes 10 minutes but I have seen people wait in long lines at quick oil change places. Customers may wait for 30-45 minutes before they get out of their vehicles to get written up. In the customers mind, however, the clock starts on their oil change once the vehicle is written up. I have observed some oil changes that took well over an hour for the service to be completed but this is rare.

- Jiffy Lube takes a team approach to servicing the customer. Consider a busy 3 bay store. They may have as many as 15 people working around the vehicles and moving from pit to pit, to keep the pace flowing. Even with this overhead, they are still efficient money makers for their owners. Service processes are simple:
  - When the customer drives up to the facility they are greeted by someone who will try to identify you as a previous customer. The customer is asked their name, year and make of vehicle and the mileage. The customer will wait in their car until the vehicle can be driven into the garage.
  - The customer will be invited to wait in the customer lounge and an employee will drive the vehicle onto the pit bay.
  - A pit guy is in a well or a pit, below the vehicle(s). They will unscrew the oil drain plug and begin draining the oil while the customer is being asked what kind of oil and additional services they would like.
  - A menu of Oil change options is presented to the customer to choose from. Customers will have a choice of a standard 10W30 for the base price, premium synthetic blends or a full synthetic. Jiffy Lube employees tell me that customers rarely choose the 10W30.
  - Once the customer makes a choice the work order is delivered to a team member who has already begun inspecting and topping off fluids. The team member will ask the pit person if the drain plug has been replaced and they will begin to install the oil and work on any other services.
  - Add on services such as; wiper blades, air filters, fuel filters, belts hoses and tire rotations are all offered. These services are performed while the vehicle is over the oil pit. The pits have scissor jacks to handle tire rotations.
  - A Technician will **always** remove the air filter and show it to the customer.
  - If the customer is receiving a flush service, coolant or transmission, the work is done over the pits. If they are very busy the vehicle may be driven off the oil pit with the flush

service performed outside. Traffic flow is constantly monitored in and out of the bays.

o   Many Jiffy Lube facilities will clean the windshield and some will even vacuum the vehicle at no additional charge.

Your customers get their oil changes done at these facilities because they believe in the need to have oil changed every 3,000 to 5,000 miles. These businesses are conveniently close to a customer's home or work. There is always a choice of products to choose from and the work is done in a relatively short period of time. The added bonus of a clean windshield or a vacuumed vehicle is a perceived bonus.

When I polled managers from these operations, they told me that the average sale was $86.00. That means they sold a lot more than an oil change and rarely had a single item repair order.

Oil and lube franchises such as Jiffy Lube, CarX, Victory Lane, Valvoline, Pennzoil, Castrol Oil are often on prime real estate with an average total building and land investment of 1.2 - 2.2 million dollars. These operations pay for themselves very quickly and many of them do not even sell brakes, batteries or tires.

Muffler Stores:

Muffler stores are not really in the muffler business any longer. Most automobile manufacturers are now using stainless steel exhaust systems. They do not rust and rarely need replacement. Muffler stores are selling maintenance and light repairs with ASE certified Technicians for all makes and models of vehicles. These stores do not handle tires for the most part. Some of them will even offer radiator repairs or heavy component work. More than not, if the work is over 3 hours they will sublet the job.

Tire Stores:

Firestone, Goodyear and Independent Tire Store operators are in business because they make money. I have heard several Dealers say "You can't make any money selling tires." If that were true retail tire stores would not have their parking lots full of your vehicles waiting for service. These stores want to do everything your shop can do, short of warranty and heavy work. Many of them will do some heavy work anyway.

Many tire stores are a one stop shop for all maintenance and light repair work on any make or model of vehicle. They have "A","B" and "C" Technicians just like a car Dealer and many of them are ASE certified. These stores offer loss-leaders to get customers into their stores. They use a one size fits all parts and pricing strategy for most repairs rather than OEM parts.

Because tire stores sell tires, there is a lift in every bay. Typically, they do not change oil in a pit. Some of the larger stores will have pits to handle large trucks and school buses. Tire price points, oil changes, brake jobs and shocks are generally the loss leaders. When you buy tires at these stores, most of the stores will rotate your tires for the life on that vehicle. Rotation labor is cheap and it keeps the customers coming back for future inspections.

Another service that tire stores focus on is alignment agreements. Essentially you overpay for the first alignment and for a year or so the customer can return to get subsequent simple thrust alignments. This will frequently lead to; shock, tie-rod and strut up sell repairs on future visits.

Nationally, the average gross margin on tires is about 18%. This a benchmark number for tire sales. Tire store managers and personnel receive bonus money for meeting volume sales projections. Tires are the bread and butter that keep customers coming in but these stores make most of their money selling all of the services that new and used car Dealers fail to sell.

Patrick W. Emmett

WalMart, K-Mart and Sears:

These stores have a distinct marketing advantage that other quick service operations do not. They have a retail shopping outlet available for the customer to entertain themselves with while the repairs are being performed. The customer waiting areas are generally quite small, by design, so the customers will spend their time shopping.

The primary focus of these quick service operations is oil changes, battery installations and tire sales. They may perform other light repair services but they will stick with what they know and they refer work that they do not do to repair shops or new car Dealers.

A major incentive for customers to buy auto service in these stores is the availability of credit card convenience. Customers will go to Sears just so they can put that tire purchase on their Sears card. Today, a hand full of banks control all but a few credit card transactions. All retailers are using branded Visa or Master Card so the incentive is not as good as it used to be.

Pep Boys, Sears and the other guys:

I was told once, that for many of the repairs performed in a Pep Boys shop, they purchase parts from other parts stores 80% of the time instead of selling from their own shelves. I don't know if this is true or not but they seem to do a brisk business with local NAPA and O'Reilly stores. I suspect that the Pep Boys stores stock for the fastest moving inventory and parts for specialized repairs would need to be supplied from a warehouse or a NAPA store.

All of these stores sell maintenance, light and medium repair service work on all makes and models of vehicles. The work is performed with a "B" or a "C" Technician. That is how they compete. They will sell remanufactured replacement parts at value prices. Pep Boys does a very brisk after-market parts operation that sell parts in the one size fits all category. They are good at what they do.

Advance and Auto Zone focus mainly on parts but I have seen some stores do offering maintenance and light component installation. One thing is for sure, if you buy a battery or even wiper blades, at one of these stores a friendly employee will install the part for you, **at no charge**. They want your business.

The after market big box service retailer offers; discounted, attention getting services, like a brake job for $89.00. The prices quoted are generally just for pad replacement, no rotor treatment for a single axel. Price leaders exclude trucks and larger vehicles. The customer is offered a good, better and best choice for most products and services. Services are generally bundled and conveniently priced. Occasionally, the Service Writer may look up labor and parts for a particular repair job but most work is sold directly off of a menu. If the repair work is too complicated, they just refer a customer to another repair facility.

General Motors Quick Service Centers:

General Motors has worked with a few Dealers to build free-standing Quick Service Centers around the country. Like most automobile manufacturers, they have trade area restrictions as to where the centers can be built and how they must look.

I have seen GM Quick Service Centers as stand alone buildings on Dealer's lots. I have seen some as facilities down the street from the dealership. I have seen GM Quick Service Centers integrated into existing dealership floor plans. GM has made it convenient for customers to obtain a quick oil change and tire service. There is little or no interest in selling brake jobs, or any other light repair work in these operations. This work is referred to the main shop Service Advisors.

GM Quick Service Centers have a write-up area and customer waiting area that is separated from the main service customer lounge in the dealership facility. Oil is changed in a shallow pit. The customer's vehicle is driven by a Technician into the service bay. A Technician will lie down on his back on a roller platform, in the pit, under the vehicle and open the drain plug. Some bays have full lifts but many are simply scissor lifts that are good enough to rotate and change tires. The shop floors are covered with an attractive non-skid rubberized tile.

There is an identifiable Goodwrench brand look to the facilities with brand color, signage and point of sale displays. The mission here is to take good care of GM customers for oil and tires, not all makes and all models. Mr. Goodwrench is no longer a promotable brand but genuine GM parts and service will continue to be at the forefront of these Quick Service franchises.

Honda:

Honda stresses the importance of a separate quick service center with their dealer body, especially in their Wave design dealerships. With Honda, everything is under one roof and basically caters primarily to Honda vehicles. Most of the work in a Honda quick service isle is for oil changes and filter replacement. Some even have oil pits installed to speed up the movement of oil changes. All other work is dispatched to the main shop.

There is a Honda Dealer in the Chicago area that has a 10 bay quick service operation that caters to all makes and models. The Service Manager has told me that even with 10 bays; they are busy all of the time. You might want to call him and ask him about his seasonal "pot-hole special."

Not all automobile manufacturers are moving toward quick service for their customers. You do not have to wait for your manufacturer to get into the business. You can take the initiative to develop your own facility and quick service brand.

CHAPTER 10

FORD QUICK LANE

What a concept! Segment oil changes and light repair work into a separate location. Provide a separate write-up area and lounge for your customers. Cater to all makes and models of vehicles. Really focus on tires for your customers. Create a recognizable brand and you have quick service that really works for your customers.

Ford Motor Co. spent a great deal of time researching the market and customer needs. They developed Quick Lane as a customer retention tool to keep vehicle buyers coming back to their dealerships again and again. I have focused on Quick Lane in this book because it is a model that works if you want to create a quick service facility at or near your dealership.

In an effort to build a quick service facility, some dealerships have gone to outside vendors and placed a variety of franchised operations into their service departments. I have seen some Dealers with a Valvoline or a Pennzoil franchise in their shops. Most Dealers just try to adapt the maintenance and light repair concept into their current operations, sparing themselves the expense of a brick and mortar add-on solution.

While working at Ford Motor Co. an enthusiastic Ford Field Manager and I visited a Dealer with the hope of selling him on the concept of building a Quick Lane. The Field Manager told the Dealer that he was looking at a ground breaking opportunity to make more money. The stunned Dealer looked back at him and said, "Oh no you don't! I do not plan to break any ground." The Field Manager kept explaining that he was just using an expression but the Dealer had already lost interest by this time. The Dealer definitely did not want to spend money on breaking any ground.

You do not have to break ground to break a trend. Your first consideration in every case is to maximize your available resources. Then after considering all options make your best choice for long term growth and convenience.

Ford Motor Co. decided to change the service paradigm in 1997. Ford was seeking greater brand loyalty from their customers while Dealers were eager to find solutions to greater fixed coverage or service absorption. Shortly before the Quick Lane program was announced, Ford instituted a program called Quality Care which was Ford's answer to GM's very successful Mr. Goodwrench brand.

Quality Care was a way to identify all of the recommended services that the vehicle owner's manual suggested at different mileage bands. Dealerships have long been enthusiastic at suggesting a customer change their oil every 3,000 miles but rarely did they recognize the need for a specific maintenance item that is recommended for any individual model of vehicle. For example, how often should a cabin air filter be replaced? When should vehicles require that a fuel filter be replaced? What about belts and hoses? All of this information is carefully logged in the owner's manual, a book that is rarely opened by customers or dealership personnel.

At the time, Ford tired to create a book with every scheduled maintenance item for every model of vehicle that they manufacture, over several years. The net result was a huge black book about a foot thick that no one could use. They even tried to automate the process. Letters were sent to customers reminding them to return to the dealership for suggested services. The process was so complicated that most dealerships did not follow the guidelines of the program and many customers received letters in the mail that made no sense at all.

Ford also introduced a program called Around the Wheel. This program was infinitely more successful. Ford chose to market tires because tire decisions are considered to be a defection point, when customers run to the aftermarket. If a customer does not return to the dealership for service why would they return to buy a new or used vehicle? So selling tires became a part of Ford's customer retention strategy.

Ford Dealers were asked to stock OEM tires for the models of vehicles that they sold. Ford negotiated discounted pricing from the various tire manufacturers and offered a "meet or beat" strategy to entice customers to come into the dealership to buy the tires. All of this worked pretty well for the Dealers and Ford Motor Co. Dealers were encouraged to offer brake, battery and tire inspections with every visit. Service departments were encouraged to inspect every vehicle, regardless of miles that came into the dealership. The whole idea was to keep the customer coming back again and again.

Dealerships made the investment. They stocked tires and they sold tires. Ford conducted contests that rewarded Service Advisors directly to move tires, brakes and batteries. Ford was convinced that warranty would decline as much as 30% and the Dealers needed to replace that revenue with Customer Pay maintenance work. Dealers often complained that maintenance work, like oil changes and tires, was low gross work and they could not make any money. While lower gross is a reality, warranty work continues to decline, the revenue needed to be replaced from somewhere..

Ford's solution to declining service revenue for Dealers was Quick Lane. If you want to improve service absorption you need to improve sales, reduce expenses, earn more gross profit, improve customer satisfaction and get more production out of your Technicians. One way to do that is to increase shop capacity and create a new profit center for the dealership, like another business.

Quick Lane allowed a Dealer to do several things that simple expansion of a conventional shop could not do:

- Improve customer satisfaction by offering convenient hours of operation that may be different from the main production shop.
- Offer the customer the convenience of a quick write-up.
- Convenience of an oil change in 30 minutes or less, and mean it!
- Customers are offered a wait while the work is being performed service experience in a comfortable lounge with bathroom facilities and refreshments. The waiting areas are separate from the main facility customer lounge. This allows for aggressive marketing of all makes and all models with a Quick Lane brand. The customer waiting area allows the customer to watch while the work is being performed on their vehicle. Instead of a car disappearing in to the back of a building for hours, the customer knows exactly what is happening to their vehicle.
- The customers are frequently invited into the Quick Lane service bays, to take a look at tires or brakes with Technicians.
- Quick Lane offers bundled service specials that simplify the write-up process with a good better and best pricing strategy.
- Quick Lane removes most of the oil changes and tire work out of the main shop. This was work that most Technicians did not want to do anyway. Technicians do scream over the perceived loss of "gravy work" but work performed in the Quick lane is work that may not have been suggested by the Technician or sold by a Service Advisor anyway. Most of the write-up business is new business to the dealership.
- By removing oil changes, tire and alignment work out of the main shop, line Technicians are able to focus on work that pays more hours. **About a year after a Quick Lane installation in Merriam Illinois, I walked through the main production shop. I was greeted with an eerie silence. I asked the Service Manager if work had fallen off in the shop. He said, "No, it looks quiet but we are actually writing more repair orders out here than ever before and our hours per repair order are also up." The production shop's gross profit, he told me, was up by quite a bit and not just because of moving a lot of the oil work to the Quick Lane.**
- The Dealer receives a better analysis of shop sales, service bay and Technician production numbers than ever before.

- Quick Lanes offer an opportunity for Dealers to expand into other profit opportunities such as accessory boutiques and detailing.
- Quick Lanes only perform work that is under 3 hours. That means that a Quick Lane Technician does not have to be Master certified. You can hire these "B" and "C" Technicians from the quick service competition down the road and offer better benefits and a career path into the main shop, to keep the cost of sale low.
- Quick Lanes are designated as an all makes all models service facility. This means that, the off-brand used vehicles you sell will return to your dealership for their maintenance services. Customers can bring all of their family vehicles into the Quick Lane and receive the same service that they can get on their Ford vehicle. Quick Lane's stock generic non-Ford parts to sell on non-Ford vehicles.
- Quick Lanes are an ideal solution for multiple franchise operators. The dealership is offering quick maintenance services to all makes and models. There is no Ford logo on the signage. Quick Lane is a brand of its own.

The concept of Quick Lane has gained traction with Ford Dealers and many of them are looking for places to open them. Some Dealers are considering the conversion of existing shop bays and add a lounge while others feel that a separate building on the main lot better serves their needs.

Many Dealers look at their struggling on site body shops as potential locations for their Quick Lanes. These Dealers realized that you can write up body work anywhere. They can move the body shop production area off site, where the environmental concerns were not quite as strict. A Dealer can build a Quick Lane anywhere on his property or with-in sight of the Ford sign, according to the terms of the Sales and Service Agreement.

Quick Lane is designed as an on-site solution to retain customers and shift work in and out of the main shop. Dealers also look down the street to other sites and locations. If the Quick Service business is down the road then you are looking at an entirely different business model.

Ford offers a unique solution called Quality Care Service Center. This is a building that could sit anywhere inside of the Dealer's trade area and offer maintenance to all makes and models of vehicles. In addition, a Quality Care Service Center could also perform some light warranty work.

Wow! Dealers thought, this is great! I can set up little service departments everywhere and be as convenient as my aftermarket competition. The fly in the ointment is that in a most markets, a Dealer would have to ask every other Ford Dealer adjacent to his market area to literally sign off on building the Quality Care Service Center. As a result, not too many Quality Care Service Centers have been built, because who wants to have the competitive Ford Dealer's service center sitting on the edge of your trade area?

Ford backed up their Quick Lane program with an aggressive follow-up campaign by well trained Quick Lane professionals. These field personnel monitor the progress of the Quick Lanes assigned to them. They make sure that the business model is working and that the brand does not veer to far from it's intended purpose. Ford offers several incentives for Dealers who engage in the Quick Lane franchise. As a result of Ford's efforts to provide a better customer service experience, Ford has become the third largest retailer of tires in the country.

Quick Lanes have become a hit and Dealers from coast to coast are including them in their dealerships all over North America today. Even if you are not a Ford franchised Dealer you can take lessons learned by what this business model has to offer and adapt it to your own.

If you are a Ford franchised Dealer, I encourage you to contact your Ford factory representative and ask them to provide you with more details on how you can create a new profit center for your dealership. Listen to them and build it right.

CHAPTER 11

WHY CUSTOMERS BUY

When people buy things they go through a decision making process. Customers consider several factors before considering which product or service to choose. Impulse buying is not as common as we would like to imagine. Customers are inundated with a lot of information. They need to filter what makes sense to them before they buy.

Researchers state that a customer goes through 4-7 stages while making a buying decision. Below are just a few:

- First the customer must become aware that a need exists.
- Information is sought for the solution of this need.
- Several alternatives will be weighed in an effort to determine the best value.
- The customer makes up their mind and chooses the good or service.
- After the purchase has been made, the customer will evaluate the experience to determine the value of the product purchased.

Service departments are in the business of constantly reminding customers of their vehicle's needs. They do this from day one when a maintenance schedule is presented to the new car buyer. They do this when the customer returns for an oil changes and services are recommended. Vehicles create need when an oil change light or a check engine light goes on.

A customer is motivated to recognize a need especially when it pertains to their basic survival. Safety needs involve self preservation and wellbeing. There are other needs too, such as social needs and personal fulfillment needs. Nothing, however, moves a customer to a decision faster than a perceived safety need.

Social networking, the media, and the internet; we as a society are awash with information. Yet, decisions are often made on the recommendation of a family member or personal friend. Consumers are bashed every day with advertising on television, radio, the internet and with print media. Frequently, there is a lot of information in these ads. If people have not become immune to the ads or products represented, they could pick up some needed knowledge to assist in their buying decision.

When a customer makes an informed decision they have to filter through several facts. That decision involves evaluating several alternatives. The customer will assess risk with factors such as cost, time, durability and value. An important part of this process is when the customer feels "involved" with the product. The product or service needs to mean something to them. You know this from selling vehicles. This is the stage where demonstrations are helpful. Point of sale materials in the service isle can frequently drive the need home concerning worn out brakes or a fouled fuel filter.

Finally, after the customer has purchased the product or service they will reflect on what they bought to determine if they, in fact, received value. It is common for customers to experience a "buyer's remorse" feeling, wondering if an alternative decision would not have served them better. If this feeling persists, it is likely that the customer will switch brands the next time. To manage this post purchase anxiety most car Dealers make a CSI follow-up phone call or contact to gage the customers' response. Typically, the customer is polled to determine if they were "completely satisfied" in order to win a high CSI score.

In Service, we look at four basic reasons why customers buy: convenience, dependability/quality, price and confidence. Customers want to take their vehicle to someone who understands and respects them. They want that business to have the knowledge and experience to work on their vehicle.

Confidence:

Customers want to develop a relationship with the people who take care of their cars. They want to know them by their first name. They want that person to know more about their vehicle than they do. They want to rely on someone else's expertise. Often, they are busy people who do not have time to become automobile experts.

A car is many things to a customer. A car is an emotional choice that they made during their first buying decision in your business. A car is an extension of the owner's personality, one of the most expensive things that person will ever buy. On the other hand, customers also think of a car as a necessary component of their lives that provides safe transportation for them and their families. They want that car to last both as an investment and as a source of dependability.

There is a false belief held by many Service Advisors, that customers do not want to spend money to take care of their vehicles. They are quick to offer discounts and cut repair items from a repair order or service menu in order to get at least some kind of a sale before that potential buyer leaves the dealership. These Service Advisors are not doing that person any favor. The customer needs to be presented with all of the options for taking care of their vehicle. Customers are people who want respect. They deserve the right to say yes or no on suggested services.

There was an advertising campaign, years ago, that stated "You can pay me now, or you can pay me later." The "later" repair is often a major repair.

That is why maintenance is such an important concept. Periodical maintenance is not a tough concept for the customer to grasp. They want the confidence that the dealership knows more about their vehicle than anyone and that the dealership is looking after that vehicle for them. They want the confidence of being treated fairly and knowing that they received value for their decision to do business with you.

Quality/Dependability:

Dependability and quality are solid reasons why customers do business with your dealership. We live in an age where someone in a back room said, **"America, you really do want cheaper imported goods to keep inflation down. You really do want to replace things frequently because when they do not last our economy will keep rolling."** And so this concept became a reality. The balance of trade between our country and other countries has shot off the charts. We are told that Americans are bargain conscious, that is good, but we need to pay attention to what we get for our money. Quality should trump quantity.

Today, everything is imported, including cheap labor. All of this is true but when you ask service customers what they want, they will tell you **they want the parts you install and the repairs you perform to last.** They want dependable parts put on by a factory trained person. They do not want to return for a repeat repair because the vehicle was not fixed right the first time. They do not want their new breaks to squeal, their wiper blades to streak or to see oil leaks on their garage floor. The customer wants the quality of OEM factory parts installed by the best talent available.

Price:

Price is not the number one reason why people buy. When a customer processes all of the facts to make an informed buying decision, quality/dependability and convenience are considered first and second. This is where the Service department needs to deliver benefits and features that emphasize safety and economy. You don't buy brakes because they are cheap!

You buy them because they will help your car stop in an emergency. You want the best brake pads you can get because your life and the lives of your precious family cargo depend on it. You don't want brakes that make needless noise. You want the brakes that were designed specifically for the operating specifications of your vehicle. You are buying brakes based on what they will do for you.

If you knew that you had to jump out of an airplane at 10,000 feet would you want the cheapest parachute money could buy or would you want the best one available with fail safe options? The point is, people do not buy price, they buy value. They buy benefits and features. Do you think the guy who sells Orrick Vacuum cleaners is selling the lowest cost or even the latest technology on the market? Absolutely not!

Price points are the ability to offer the customer choices to make their decision process easier. If you can offer the customer a tiered choice for what they are looking for, you have a better chance of doing business with that person. Bundled choices are an excellent way to allow the customer to make an easy decision between A, B or C. Any more than three alternatives tends to confuse the buyer.

Bundled choices should be offered on service menus. Just bundling some services for full retail mark-up and printing them on paper will not sell them. Customers need to perceive value for their purchases. What are they getting for their money and why? By offering choices and reasons to buy, you will sell many additional services at full retail mark-up, if the customer sees the benefit, that is. You certainly would not sell a car without explaining the benefits and features, service is no different.

Wal-Mart offers a large variety of batteries for sale. They have huge displays in their isles to sell batteries. How much do you think the average Wal-Mart customer pays for a battery? Most people I ask generally respond with $39.95. That price is the entry level that gets people in the door. I have been told by a former Wal-Mart auto service store managers that the average battery sale is $89.00 or even higher. That means a lot of batteries over $100.00 are sold. People do not want to put a cheap or "beater" battery into their better car. Price points can be loss leaders to get the customer in the door but you sell the customer what they feel that they want and need, a decision they make with good information.

The concept of price points, offers specific pricing for specific applications or fitment. For example, if you were to run a tire ad; do you promote "tires from $89.00 and up?" Or do you run a special on a popular brand of tire with a break-down of sizes? This allows a potential buyer to find the size and price on tires for their vehicle. Tire stores run their ads and list several tires with sizes and prices for each size. As a car Dealer, you could even be more specific and name the vehicle product that the tires fit on. Customers can relate to that. Customers cannot always relate to a 235x70R16. They can relate to "We have tires for your Ford Explorer – 235x70 R16, only $89.00 each!

The Concept of Convenience:

Convenience is a customers' perception of how easy it is to do business with you. Convenience can be interpreted as time. People want to visit a business that is close to their home or work, with longer hours of operation so they can come in before or after work. More importantly, they don't want to wait in long lines.

Convenience for a service customer is someone who will answer the phone when they call to make an appointment. You can extend hours of operation, provide quick write-ups and delivery. You can extend value when you wash their car and get the work done quickly. In some cases, you can provide a shuttle to the Mall or a ride to work. All things are possible when you look at what your customers needs are and think of convenience as time.

Location is often confused with convenience. You cannot move your facility to be with-in 2-3 miles of your customer base, so you have to provide other reasons for them to come in.

Most after market quick service facilities are open from 7:00 AM to 7:00 PM, Monday through Friday. Saturday hours are typically 8:00 AM to 5:00 PM. Many oil and tire stores are also open to do business on Sunday from noon to 5:00 PM. What are your hours?

After market providers do not staff a parts department on week-ends and they do not pay Cashiers to print tickets. They do not offer shuttles and they do not have service loaners. After market quick service operations make efficient use of their personnel. Technicians in the after market, have easy access to parts. The person who wrote up the customer concern will cashier the customer when the work is complete. To a customer, all of this translates into time which is convenience.

Convenience is also the ability to drive up, be recognized, and be served quickly. Customers find it annoying to wait in line for anything, especially automotive service. Quick service facilities that allow the customer to drive up get out of their car, and go into a waiting room for a write-up are perceived to be better served. Customers also like the write-up process which is quick and as painless as possible with the use of menus and quick choices.

Convenience is having credit card applications available for your customers. If a customer needs tires or has a major repair decision to make, the decision could be a lot easier with a new line of credit. There are several card companies out there who will work with you on this project.

A quick turn-around for repairs is an important convenience consideration. The speed with which the requested repairs can be completed will improve customer perceptions. Getting work in and out of the shop quickly can depend on the number of bays available, how many Technicians you have to do the work and how quickly they can access parts. Most dealerships are not structured to accommodate a smooth and seamless quick service process flow.

CHAPTER 12

BUILDING YOUR OWN
QUICK SERVICE BUSINESS

The notion of incorporating some form of quick service into new car dealerships is nothing new. The concept has been around since the first car rolled off an assembly line. Over the years, the service delivery experience has changed little with the demand for more specialized work, factory trained Technicians and tons of warranty work. As cars became more complex, Technicians began to be paid on a flat rate, where they would "clean the ticket." Most Technicians, 30 years ago, would complete all of the repair lines on a dispatched ticket. Many shops today continue to operate this way.

Even in a specialized shop today, it's not uncommon for a Master Technician to work all of the concerns on a ticket. So you find them doing an oil change and tire rotation on a fuel pump replacement ticket. Master Technicians do brake jobs, because they can turn that hour and a half job, in less than a half hour and pocket the money billed on the time. This bonus for working fast is called "gravy." The Dealer has just paid the most expensive Technician in the shop to perform a task with the least skill necessary. Where is the Dealer's gravy?

In order to make more money, improve traffic flow in the shop, and help with customer satisfaction, Dealers are looking at separating many of the repairs that can be called quick services in their shops. Light repairs are separated and all repair work is assigned based on the appropriate skill levels to Technicians. We are in an emerging age of de-specialization of the shop.

If you think about it, Technicians rarely repair transmissions or any major components any longer. They replace them with new or remanufactured components. Drivability and electronic issues are the jobs that take the longest to repair and have the highest level of customer concern. These repairs require computers and years of training. These are the jobs that need Technicians with a mindset for solving puzzles. This is where a Dealer wants his highest skilled Technicians working, not changing air filters. You want your diesel Technician solving problems, not looking for wiper blades.

I frequently perform 100 Repair Order studies on Customer Pay tickets for Dealers. What I look for on those tickets, among other things, is the age and mileage of vehicles as well as trends. What always stands out is the sheer number of one item repair orders. Most of them are an LOF (Lube, Oil and Filter). Generally, over 50% of those reviewed are single item repair orders. In states with vehicle inspections that number can go up to 80%.

Oil changes are the repair orders that will clog up the scheduling and loading to Technicians in most Service departments. These repair orders frequently mean that someone is waiting in the customer lounge for their vehicle. Customers have learned that when the vehicle is written up and it disappears into the back of the shop they may not see their car any time soon. Four hour oil changes are not uncommon in our business. That is the primary reason why customers will not ask to have any additional Customer Pay work performed when they come in for a basic oil change. Customers have learned that to add any repair or service will take an incredible amount of time for someone to diagnose, let alone a repair.

So, here is the paradigm, you want to improve the way you do business with your service customers, but what do you do? Creating a quick service solution for your shop solves a lot of issues with work flow and customer satisfaction. There are many ways to approach quick service opportunities for your business.

Some Dealers pick a bay or two, hire a couple of $8.00 an hour guys and do oil changes all day long in those bays to address quick service. This action will moves the bulk of the customer pay tickets oil tickets out of the production shop. The dealer is managing low grossing oil changes and the high volume of tickets but several other problems creep up when you do this. For example, how skilled are $8.00 guys at finding additional maintenance work? Can they rotate tires? How do you sell wiper blades, batteries and filters in this model? If you do not rotate the tires how do you recommend a replacement set of tires or even brakes?

Customers tell me that they want to watch the work being performed on their vehicle. This is not possible when work is sent into the main shop, out of the customer's view.

For many Dealers this is their complete solution. Quick service of this type has few opportunities for up-selling additional maintenance services. Still, the separation of the oil changes out of the shop did speed up basic oil changes for the customer and shop loading can be streamlined.

A measurement tool used to calculate how oil changes affect your overall shop performance is "hours per customer pay repair order." To calculate your dealerships average **"hours per customer pay repair order", take the total month-end customer pay sales from the financial statement and divide this number by the total customer pay repair orders for that month, then divide that number by either the true customer pay effective labor rate or the door rate if the effective labor rate is unknown.** The door rate will generally calculate to fewer hours per repair order. When Dealers analyze their hours per customer pay repair orders, they are often shocked when they see hours per repair order at 1.1 or 1.5. A good goal is 3 or more.

Some Service Managers will try to remove oil changes from calculations on their effective labor rate. They do this because the Dealer is looking at the numbers. If you do that you are just kidding yourself. Oil changes are a part of the business and you need to include them to get a real picture. There are better ways to improve your effective labor rate and your hours per repair order than by manipulating oil change statistics.

If your hours per customer pay repair order are under 2 hours per repair order on average, you have work to do in your Service department. You can make no excuses for the number of oil changes that your business does. You should be happy that your customers are returning to you with their business. What you may not be doing is capitalizing on the revisit opportunity with your customers when they return. If all you are selling them is an oil change (LOF) then you have an incredible opportunity to do a better job. The problem you then have is convincing those customers to stay around to get other services performed. This is tough, because of the poor expectation customers have for getting work performed conveniently and quickly.

Some Dealers have chosen to re-create the experience that their customers enjoy at competitive establishments. Business such as PEP Boys, Firestone, Goodyear, Jiffy Lube, Midas, CarX and Tuffy have all made their names by providing quick, efficient and convenient services that customers can depend on.

Typical gross for quick service facilities is about 65% on labor. Parts can gross 28% or better even with tires added in. I have seen tire gross profit percentage average any where from 11% to 28%, depending on the market and type of tires commonly sold. Departmental gross can also be improved by Dealers who offer after market parts and accessories for add-on services.

How regressive is it, to send all of your used vehicle trades and auction cars down the street to a competitor for reconditioning? I know, I have heard all of the arguments. Used Car Managers complain that the parts department marks up the parts too much and that the service department simply cannot get the vehicles through the shop in a reasonable amount of time. Managers believe that a used vehicle has a finite amount of gross and the service department will erode that gross.

Dealers who condone this behavior are cheating themselves out of gross. The creation of a quick service operation would allow you to move some or all of the used vehicle reconditioning into a lower cost production model. If you do this, however, be sure to charge the full door rate and full parts mark-up on your internal tickets. Remember what your shop labor and parts grosses are? Believe me; the Used Car department will get their share of gross on vehicles sold. That is how they get paid. Pay yourself first.

Dealers who routinely perform all reconditioning in their own shop get paid their gross first through their fixed operations department.

The primary reason for moving maintenance and light repair to a quick service operation is customer retention. Your customers will return to buy vehicles from you if they feel like they have been treated well in your service department. They want a well informed, pleasant write-up experience with service that is fast and addresses their needs. They want someone knowledgeable looking out for their vehicle. Customers do not want a painful encounter that may cause them to defect to another car Dealer.

Just giving away a free first oil change is not enough to keep your customers coming back to you for return visits. Warranty is the only leverage you have to keep your new car customers loyal. You have to do a better job of giving the customer reasons to return to your service department. If you can provide; quick service, hours of operation, price points, courteous employees, an informative write-up experiences, your customers will return again and again. You will continue to see that customer once their vehicle goes out of warranty. Customers want to feel like you know them and their vehicle, they want a reason to return.

Another reason to consider quick service is that Dealers who have built one see their gross profits in service go up. Adding more maintenance will have the effect of slightly lowering your total gross percent but, gee wiz, you are more than making up the dollars in volume output and streamlining shop operations. In other words, you will make more money.

Patrick W. Emmett

CHAPTER 13
QUICK SERVICE
WHAT YOU NEED TO CONSIDER

Let's say that you have made up your mind to create a quick service operation in your dealership. Perhaps you have a vision as to how you want it to look. Before you sign that construction contract there are a few things to consider.

The first thing that needs to take place, is to create an environment for change in your business. You would be ill advised to just spring this concept on your employees. Buy-in is necessary to be successful. If you are a Dealer or a key manager, often, the buck stops with you. As a decision maker, you need to remember that you have hired others in your organization to assist you with delegation of business policy. Trust these people to help you now.

Some Dealers make decisions, lay them on the table and demand that these decisions be implemented. You know, "My way or the highway." After all, that was how most of us learned the business. You may get the desired results you want for awhile, or not.

The other way, is to create an environment of shared guided discovery. Hold a meeting with your key employees. Ask them to brainstorm with you. Use open ended questions that lead them to where you are going. Tell them what your ultimate goals are, like making more gross profit, improving fixed coverage or adding a quick service to your business. Techniques like this will often generate better results because the employees have a vested interest in seeing their ideas come into reality. I am not suggesting you all sit around and sing Kyumbaya but it pays to listen. These are the people that are going to make your dream happen. They have good ideas and they need to be thinking the same as you.

The next challenge is to create a culture of really wanting to take care of your customers in your dealership. Your employees must feel, each day, when they come to work, that their mission is to help your customers. They need to be prepared to drop everything and walk a customer through your store to their destination. They need to remember to smile and look like they mean it. They need to be proactive and ask customer's questions about how they are doing, how they like their vehicle or what can be done to make their visit more comfortable. These are just the courtesies that you expect when you visit any business.

A positive customer experience is a key reason to build a quick service operation. In doing so, you are presenting the customer with a new set of alternatives from those they may have previously received at your dealership. Creating a new culture is so important because it translates into something you are very fond of, profits.

As I stated earlier in the book, if you are in business for any other reason than profit, then this book is probably not for you. The primary reason for separating your quick service operation from your main shop is so that your most expensive cost of labor employee is not performing the least profitable work. Dealership service production shops need to be in the business of producing more billable hours for more complex work at a higher effective labor rates. Most quick services can be performed by a less skilled work force at a lower cost of sale.

You need to keep in mind that when you separate your quick service operation from your main shop, you will be increasing the volume of those quick services. Your repair order count in oil changes, rotations, brake jobs, flushes, wiper and filter replacements, tires sales and alignments will go up. The more added maintenance items you sell above an oil change will determine how much gross profit you make on each ticket. Even with an exceptional sales job of additional maintenance labor operations on quick service tickets, your gross profit will not be as high as your current average shop ticket.

When I was a 20 Group Moderator we would review everyone's financials in the group. There was always a Dealer in the group whose service gross profit percentages were outstanding. Dealers would discuss process and cost of labor and work to assist Dealers whose numbers were the lowest. I remember one Dealer who always had the highest total service gross. The Dealers were enviable. They all wanted to know how he did it, until they looked at his volume. His Service Manager and Parts Manager squeezed high gross profit out of their sales because that was how they got paid, but they had very few sales to show for their effort. In other words, all retail services were offered at full retail mark-up. No discounts, specials or bundling strategies were used to entice customers to buy in this store. This Dealer was paying his people on percent goals and loosing money on his service operation due to low volume, in a big way.

So keep in mind that you might have to rearrange some pay plans here and there. Your service operations will be more efficient and your customers will be delighted with the changes you make. You will make more money even if the total gross profit percent appears lower on the balance sheet.

Each of the following categories should be reviewed while making your quick service decision. Some of these considerations will make sense to you and others you will throw out. This information comes from years of working with businesses to improve their service operations. Glean what you need.

Inspections:

Every quick service facility performs vehicle inspections. They may be 18 point inspections or more. I have even seen 56 point inspections. What ever you choose to do, be consistent and perform them on *all* vehicles, *all* of the time. No exceptions! This will build customer confidence, that you really understand what is going on with their vehicle.

I remember when dealerships used manual repair orders. Many of them had a diagram on the back so that the Service Advisor could perform a cursory inspection while they wrote-up the customers concerns. The inspections were used to determine if there was any prior physical damage done to the vehicle. This was done to limit the liability of the Dealer while that vehicle was in the shop. Over time, Dealers took those inspections a step further, to check for oil leaks, check belts, fluids, wiper blades and to look for tail light failures while the customer was in the dealership. Of course in those days gas stations provided many of the same services, at no charge. Those days have disappeared along with tail fins and pony tails.

Today, most manufacturers have jumped on board the vehicle inspection train. They are all buying into the concept that vehicle inspections are tied to customer satisfaction and customer satisfaction interprets into customer loyalty and that results in more new vehicles sold for that manufacturer and car Dealer. Every factory has put their spin on what the inspection form should look like. In one case, the manufacturer developed as many a 4 types of inspection forms that could be used on vehicles coming through the shop. The choices were so confusing; most Service Advisors didn't bother to use them at all.

In an effort to encourage Dealers to get on board with the inspection process, manufacturers have offered a variety of incentives and pay-back plans. Some have even installed a system of punishments for a Dealer's failure to comply with inspections. Regardless of what your manufacturer provides, the concept is solid. Use it!

When I perform 100 repair order studies, the most common inspection failure is selective inspections. Service Advisors or the Technicians take it upon themselves to choose which vehicles will get an inspection. Judgments like these often overlook vehicles which would have benefited the most from an inspection.

A few dealerships ask permission from the customer before they perform an inspection. Sometime in the past they got burned when some customer said that they did not want an inspection. If you are afraid your customers might object to an inspection, post it on the wall! **"We will provide a courtesy vehicle inspection on every vehicle serviced at this facility."** When asked about the policy by your customers, stress the safety factor of driving with brakes that stop, shocks that work and tires that won't blow a tread because of a nail or bead wear . Let them know you care about them and their families and that you are looking out for their vehicle. If they decline, ask them to sign the inspection form.

Some dealerships attach an inspection form to every ticket that is dispatched to the shop. This is a good start. My studies reveal, that both the customer copy and the file copy wind up being attached to the work order. This is alright as long as the Technician completes the inspection process. The customer copy can later be detached and handed to the customer with a copy of the paid invoice.

The process breaks down when inspection paperwork is stapled and absolutely nothing is checked or marked on the forms, indicating that an inspection was not performed. I think dealerships are trying to be compliant with some factory program by attaching the inspection forms to every ticket and not completing them. Keep in mind, that those forms are not free. The dealership has paid for them. Even though they are sent from the factory, there is a cost associated with them, sometimes as much as seventy five cents apiece for multiple part forms. That is just money down the drain if they are not properly used. How many dollars in sales do you have to make to cover that foolish net loss?

Another inspection donnybrook, that I have observed, is when inspection forms are attached to every ticket but Technicians just draw a line through all of the items to be inspected. A decision is made, for example, on 3,000 mile vehicles to not inspect. The thinking here is that there could not possibly be anything wrong with the vehicle. In fact, some 3-15,000 mile vehicles do have unusual tire wear. Low mileage vehicles do have poorly charged batteries and they do have unusual use of under the hood fluids that could all indicate more serious problems. The practice of drawing a line through inspection boxes shows up on vehicles of all mileage ranges, however. Failure to inspect every vehicle, every time, will result in problems for your customers!

There is nothing wrong with inspecting a 3-15,000 mile vehicle and giving that customer the vote of confidence that everything is still okay and someone is looking out for them. In the long run you will have that vehicle coming back again and again for future work.

The biggest single roadblock, to universal vehicle inspections in dealerships, is the Technician. Every shop has some Technicians who do everything they can to do the right thing. They believe that if they inspect vehicles they may find additional work. If they owned an independent shop, I can guarantee you that they would go over every vehicle they saw with a fine tooth comb. Unfortunately, in a lot of shops, there are Technicians who are only looking for one thing, the next work order. Let the Technicians in your shop know you mean business. These guys are costing you money.

Many dealerships only inspect vehicles on customer pay repair orders over 15,000 miles or under 80,000 miles and never on a diesel vehicle. My belief is that if the Service Advisor or dispatcher needs to think about which vehicles get inspections and which ones do not, the process will fail. Inspect every vehicle that comes through your shop. That means every customer pay ticket every warranty customer and every internal ticket, regardless of miles.

If your shop is reconditioning used vehicles, you know all too well that, your Technicians can do a pretty good job of inspections. They seem to find virtually anything that can go wrong on your recently acquired used inventory for an internal ticket. Make no exceptions! Inspect every vehicle.

Charging for inspections is silly. Some Dealers charge a fee to cover the cost of paying a Technician to perform the inspection. Keep in mind; this is how *you* make *your* money and how the Technician makes his money. Your Technicians really need to inspect the vehicles they work on and look for things that need to be replaced or repaired.

When Technicians do perform an inspection they may say, that they are too busy to check for PCV valves, fuel filters, wiper blades, belts, hoses and even air filters. They make this complaint for one simple reason, they get paid on labor hours turned, not on parts sold. The working theory here is that Technicians will look for replacement parts because they get paid to put them on. I have talked to many Technicians who consider maintenance parts replacement an annoyance.

If you want a real wake-up call, go out to your Service department and collect the closed customer pay tickets once a week and look them over. First look to see if there was an inspection performed then look at the miles. Check to see if anything was recommended and finally if anything was sold. No doubt, you will be shocked by your findings. My advice is, do not go back to your Service department and shout "Off with their heads!" You are better served by reviewing your processes and compensation plans. More than not, you will discover that employees will do just what they get paid to do, no more, no less.

Oil:

Oil, like tires, is a primary reason that people come in to your business for service. There is a perception that people want the lowest cost oil in their vehicles. This is false. I hear Dealers declaring that they are offering $9.95 oil changes to drive customer pay traffic into their dealerships. My answer to that is, $9.95 to $19.95 does not even cover the Dealers cost of oil.

All these promotions do is attract people with "beater" vehicles who want nothing more than a cheap oil change and an oil filter. The dealership becomes so busy turning oil changes during these campaigns, that there is no chance to up-sell any other services. This practice is a waste of time for everyone at the dealership and it costs you money. If you want to get into the charity business, offer free oil changes to churches and Red Cross vehicles. At least, you will get the write-off and a lot of good press.

Charge a fair price for your oil and filter change. For most vehicles, an oil change is a 5 quarts of oil at $39.95 for 10w30 oil and an inexpensive filter. $39.95 is an entry level price point at most Jiffy Lube stores. The price goes up from there, $49.95 for a synthetic blend is average and up to $80 for a 100% synthetic oil change. Charge a fair price for your oil service. Keep in mind that along with gasoline prices, the cost of oil is going up as well. Soon, your price for an oil change will need to reflect market trends.

Oil changes prices for trucks and larger vehicles, is higher because you are using more oil. Diesel vehicles are charged more as well. Pricing should not be static. Consider offering choices to all of your customers. Tier your oil price choices, print them out and stick with them.

The lesson learned here is, if you want to provide your customers with a reason to come in, do not lower the cost of your oil change. Provide some other benefit to your customers such as a **FREE tire rotation and a 21 point inspection.** Give the customer an opportunity for you to get the vehicle up on a lift rack so you can inspect the brakes, shocks, CV Boots, search for leaks and look for tread wear and nails in the tires. This is good information for the customer and is perceived as a real value. Some dealerships are offering Oil Change and Car Wash packages to bring customers in the door. That works too but you are not gaining any under the car sales from a car wash.

What kinds of oil do you offer for your customers? Most automotive manufacturers frown on using any oil other than the factory brand in the shop. For vehicles under warranty, this is a reasonable expectation. Vehicles who visit a quick service facility might want other choices. As long as you are offering the factory recommended oil for warranty repairs in your main shop and in you quick service facility, you should be compliant. Other choices such as Pennzoil, Castrol, Valvoline, Mobil One and other brands should be made available to quick service customers because they ask for them. You can address your multiple oil offerings with case oil rather than bulk oil.

Oil is not cheap, so it is in your best interest to negotiate your best deal on any oil contract from your oil supplier. Review your contract frequently. Look around; there are several oil distributors in every Dealer's trade area. Be prepared to offer at least two and better yet, three grades of bulk oil for your customers. Buy your transmission fluid and washer fluid in bulk as well, to save money. By buying these fluids in bulk you are in a much better negotiating position for a better price from your oil supplier than if you purchased them piecemeal.

Watch long term commitments to your oil supplier and be wary of kick back's in the form of an advertising bonus. Your cost of oil just went up if you took that bonus up front. You may get some kind of a check in the beginning but your daily operating cost of sale will increase and you will lower your gross profit margin. These advertizing schemes will skew what you are really making in your Parts department and quick service facility.

State Inspections:

Some states are very aggressive about requiring annual vehicle inspections. In New York State, for example, I was surprised by the sheer number of state inspections that were performed in dealership Service departments. I have to give the dealerships in that state credit. Generally, they found something to fix on just about every vehicle, so that the customer could get certified for another year. Some of the inspections yielded quite a bit of service work to be performed. I guess we can all feel a little safer driving on New York roads, knowing that the vehicles are as dependable as law and personal income will allow.

In some states, the inspection process is simply a rubber stamp so that the customer can get a renewed car tag. Most of these inspections only take a couple of minutes and the charge is a small fee. Customers come in for the inspections and no other work is performed. The net effect to the dealership is additional overhead and an increase in customer pay repair orders. Low cost inspections also lowers the gross profit percent average on all customer pay business.

Counting state inspections as a customer pay repair does not make sense. It would be helpful if the Dealer Systems Providers provided a labor type of "S" for State Inspection as a sale code. This would categorize the sale properly. I have seen some Dealers write up state inspections as an internal labor operation, to keep their customer pay numbers in line. State inspections are still a revenue stream for the dealership and state governments require them. You would be wise to find a way to properly accounted for them.

Tires:

Most tire manufacturers claim that 60% of customers will buy tires from the first service agent who asks them. Yet, many Dealers are reluctant to get into the tire business. Tires are the one service item most people feel good about spending money on. Tires are a tangible commodity. You can kick, feel and smell them. There is the assurance that your family will be safer on new rubber. Consumers want safety, performance and fuel economy from their tire purchases and now, they want the style of a good looking tire on big rims.

When you go to a franchised tire store they will inventory no fewer than 400-500 tires. In a tire store the tire manufacturer sends tires to the store based on two formulas, sales history of certain tire models and sizes and what is selling nationally. Tire store Managers can control an inventory this size. DOT dates are tracked and tires are routinely returned to their manufacturers' warehouse to keep the inventory fresh.

Do tires have a lifespan and a shelf life? Currently, there is a great deal of controversy surrounding the notion that tires have a shelf life. Information is available that suggest tires should sit on a shelf not more than 3-5 years. The chemistry of the tires changes over time and the oils tend to evaporate leaving the strength of the tire in question. It pays to move your inventory quickly but if you have old tires and cannot exchange them with your supplier, you might want to cut your losses.

Ford Motor and Chrysler have taken a stand by publishing, in owner's manuals, that customers should not retain tires on their vehicles more than six years. When it comes to the age of a tire, the tire industry takes the position that road wear and mileage have more to do with how well a tire holds up. Their point that most tires wear out before they age out is common sense. If you want to determine just how old tires are, you can always consult the DOT on the tires themselves.

The US Department of Transportation (DOT) requires that tire identification numbers be a combination of the letters DOT followed by ten, eleven or twelve letters and/or numbers to identify a manufacturing location, tire size and manufacturer's code. Since the year 2000 the week and year the tire was manufactured will be the last four numbers in this series with two for the week and two for the year appearing on the tire. A number on a tire that reads, DOT EJ8J DFM *287* is interpreted as; manufactured in the 28th week of the 7th year of the decade.

Most car Dealers who are in the car business have discovered that when the tires are delivered, you own them. Rarely does a Dealer have any return privileges for choosing the wrong tires. There is no return privilege to many suppliers on tires for a customer who did not show up to have them installed. Tires are sometimes delivered for a used vehicle that was just sold off the lot, before the tires arrived at the dealership. I knew one Dealer who always replaced tires on arriving new diesel pick-up trucks because he preferred a specific brand and size for these models. As a result, he had a shed full of new take-off tires that he could not sell. All of these things and more can happen. When they do, tire inventories can grow out of control.

Automobile manufacturers have not helped. They have negotiated deals with most of the tire companies for OEM replacement tires. When vehicles hit your lot they may have Firestone, Goodyear, Pirelli, or Kumo on them. So, which tires do you stock? Some tires are just hard to get from the tire manufacturer or distributor. Your best bet is to take a deposit and tell the customer that their tires will be delivered from your warehouse (the tire distributor).

You cannot stock all tires that may be demanded by your customers. Your customers may come in with a vehicle that has non-OEM tires. This is especially true if they show up in a make and model not offered by your dealership. You look the tires up and get a surprise to discover that they do not have the same discount structure as your OEM offerings. You cannot be all things to all customers but you too can shop around for the customer in an effort to retain them.

Generally, automobile factory programs have negotiated a pretty good deal for Dealers to take advantage on OEM tires across their vehicle product lines. When your customers compare similar tires at a discount retail stores it looks like your tires cost more. Big box stores are not offering the exact same tire you are offering. The speed rating could be different, the chemical content and performance rating could be different even though you may be comparing the same brand of tire.

Remember, when the automobile manufacturer installs tires at the factory they do so for a specific vehicle fitment (make and model of vehicle). These are the tires that meet new vehicle engineering specifications to perform within published tolerances. When you put anything else on the vehicle you change that formula and the vehicles' performance and safety standards may change. This is true with rims of different sizes as well as tires.

Companies like TCI tire distributors, are very good about replacing inventory that has not sold. They will work with the Dealer to help keep the inventory fresh and deliver tires that represent a value to your customers and more profit to you. There are several options out there, look for your best supply outlet. Some automobile manufacturers require that you purchase all of your tires through their program.

The tire industry will tell you that most vehicle roll-over accidents are due to under inflation of the tire and tread wear, not a design flaw of the tire.

Automobile manufacturers will tell you that there was no design flaw in the vehicle as well. Customers make decisions to change tire sizes and rim sizes. They may not know what they are doing. This is another good reason to inspect every tire that comes through a quick service facility.

It is startling how many foreign objects can be pulled out of tires from glass to nails. Processes such as "Chalk Talk" work. I watched a tire consultant walk into a typical car dealership and capture the attention of every Technician in the shop. He did this with a simple piece of chalk. He would walk up to any vehicle sitting on a lift rack in the shop and invite the Technicians to watch him. He would mark a chalk line across a tire then rotate it about 10-12 inches inspecting the grooves and tread wear. As he was doing so he would occasionally find a screw, nail, a piece of glass or some other foreign object imbedded into the tire tread.

"Now is the time" he would say, "to invite the customer out to see their tires." At other times he would just suggest that the Technician remove the tire, repair it and place the nail or screw into a plastic bag and attach that bag to the work order. A repair is done if the repair was simple and there was no other tread wear on the tire. The work is performed at no charge to the customer and the customer is handed the plastic bag with the foreign object in it. How much customer confidence was gained when that was done? You cannot buy advertising as good as what that customer will do for the dealership over the next few weeks and months. I have seen everything from screw drivers to pliers pulled out of tires. It is amazing what you can find. I was at a dealership and witnessed a live round of ammunition being carefully extracted from a tire. Take care of your customers, inspect tires thoroughly.

Nitrogen Sales:

Car Dealers have shied away from offering Nitrogen in tires to their customers on the service isle. I hear reasons like the cost of the equipment was too high or they just do not believe in the science of adding more nitrogen to tires.

78% of the air you breathe is composed of nitrogen. The atomic number of nitrogen is 7. The nitrogen molecules are larger than the molecules of regular air in a tire. The claim of the Nitrogen industry is that the air will not seep out of the tires as easily when they are inflated with nitrogen, up to 98% in purity. This means the tire will stay inflated longer and will be safer on the road. Better inflated tires will wear longer, reduce roll-overs and earn better gas mileage. When air is compressed into a tire some of the air literally condenses into water in the tire. This water will slush around in tires and eventually can seep through the bead and corrode the rims causing even more air leaks and this presents a potential safety hazard. Freeze thaw conditions degradate the lining of the tire, creating tire wear from with-in.

NASCAR uses nitrogen in tires. The military uses nitrogen in tires. The airlines use nitrogen in passenger airplane tires. Why would you not want to provide nitrogen to your customers?

When you sell tires there are two add on services that always make sense; an alignment and nitrogen inflation for the longevity of the tire. Offering nitrogen on the quick service isle is also a great customer retention tool. Customer feel compelled to return to your business for nitrogen air fill-ups and checks from time to time. With oil changes increasing from every 3,000 miles to 5 or 8,000 miles your service cycle has been expanded. Nitrogen gives the customer another reason to come and visit you.

Companies like NitroFill and Purigen98 have complete customer retention packages that customers can buy that include Road Side Assistance. You can sell the Nitrogen ala carte or as a package deal in your menu. Offering nitrogen is another great profit tool that works.

There are many car Dealers who pre-fill all tires on their new and used car lots with nitrogen. The vehicle department markets and sells this as an added benefit for doing business at the dealership.

Selling nitrogen service and subsequent fills on the service isle is an additional profit opportunity. Offering free nitrogen fill-ups and checks with each set of new tires also keeps customers returning. Costco does this, why can't you?

Creating a Quick Service Ticket:

Invoicing software has always been a bottleneck for most quick service facilities in dealerships. In order to keep accounting simple, quick service facilities have had to use the cumbersome service invoicing and parts sales screens from their dealer computer systems providers to write up a customer. Unfortunately, a quick service write-up may require the writer to visit as many as 5 different screens in some dealer management systems (DMS).

One or two of the DMS companies have just recently developed a single screen write-up program where a customer can be added, the 3 C's recorded and parts sold and the entire transaction invoiced with a receipt. One screen, one step. The accounting is made to the dealerships General Ledger for the Quick Service department, the Service department or anywhere you want to point the sales and cost of sales.

Aftermarket software is available for quick service write-up. This alternative to DMS software comes with some drawbacks. The write-up process is simplified. Often people are hired from the aftermarket to run the quick service facilities and many of them are already familiar with these programs. The fly in the ointment is, the awkward way accounting is tracked for this new profit center in the dealership. Relief of parts inventory and interfacing that with the DMS inventory is also a burden. Even though some Dealers have migrated to outside stand-alone software solutions to handle quick service most choose to stay with their DMS software, thereby keeping their Office Manager happy.

The main problems associated with using aftermarket software is tied to parts inventory control and accounting interfaces with the dealerships DMS provider. Using DMS software may be difficult to use for the quick service advisors but your dealership will have a more familiar system of accountability for a Quick Service department.

Most DMS providers will allow you to set up a separate accounting and service invoicing division in their software. This will allow you to use a unique chart of accounts for the quick service operation and the ability to track a separate quick service parts inventory. You should also set up a numbering scheme that is different for your quick service invoices from your main shop. With this set-up you will be able to run a separate DOC (Daily Operating Control) and trial balance for your quick service operation. At the end of the month your accounting department should merge your numbers into the dealerships general ledger.

Accounting:

Most Dealers have agreed that accounting for a quick service operation should be separate from the main dealership. The purpose for a separate set of account numbers is to gain accurate accounting information on the performance of the business as a stand alone operation. The numbers can be merged later in the month before the books are closed and pointed to the "Other Sales" box on the balance sheet or simply merged into the total customer pay labor and parts lines on your statement.

When choosing account numbers, it is wise to track the sales, cost of sales and expenses with different account numbers from the main dealerships chart of accounts. I suggest altering familiar account numbers with an additional digit on the end. Use accounting schedules to track expenses, receivables and other key items. The altered account numbers will ultimately be pointed to where ever you want your quick service operation to show up on your financial statement. Reporting and accountability help make your quick Service department stand out as a single piece of the whole dealership.

Hours of Operation:

If you are considering a quick service facility, you need to think of how your competition works this business model. The typical quick service facility is open from 7:00 AM to 7:00 PM Monday through Friday. Saturday the doors go open at 8:00 AM and close around 5:00PM. Many are open on Sunday from 12:00 PM to 5:00 PM.

In order for you to be competitive, you will need to match many of the hours offered by the other service facilities in your community. The best way to get a grasp of what they are doing is to simply visit those stores and note the times when they are open.

Your customers want to come into your business when it is convenient for them. They want to visit your dealership when they are not working. This means that you will need to schedule some shifts that are different from your main shop. In all likelihood, you will need to double up on people in the early morning and evening hours. Noon can be a busy time for quick service as well. Business can slack off in the afternoon. Week-ends require more attention because that is when the typical quick service customer will shop for tires and get maintenance work performed.

Fleet service customers want to have quick service work performed during the evenings and week-ends too. They are busy during the 8:00 AM to 5:00 PM hours and they cannot afford to take a vehicle out of service just to change oil and get tires rotated. They want to come in and have their work performed when they are not making money. This is an important segment of business that is often overlooked by many service departments, but if you take good care of your commercial customers they will be very loyal.

In an effort to keep quick service Technicians busy during the afternoon, many dealers have opted to dispatch internal work to the quick service department. This helps the Dealer control cost of labor on the work and the turn-around time for used vehicles to the sales lot is generally a lot quicker.

When you visit other quick service operations, it looks like there are no cars in the oil change lifts at all. You may well wonder how they stay open. The employees appear to be busy using a broom or a hose to clean-up during these times. Keep in mind that customers arrive in droves and clusters. This is hard to predict but this business definitely has times when you get "slammed" and when you just seem idle.

Handling of parts is a consideration for hours of operation. If you are going to be open at times when your parts department is not open, you will need to make some accommodations. Most quick service operations maintain an inventory of quick moving parts on hand. For some light repairs, parts may need to be purchased from a parts store that is open when your quick service operation is open and your dealership parts department is not. It really does not make sense to keep a parts employee on hand Saturday and after hours for a quick service operation. Watch the parts being purchased on the outside and then have your Parts Manager make a determination as to which parts should be inventoried in the quick service operation.

Parts Management:

As mentioned above, it is advisable to maintain an inventory of fast moving maintenance and light repair parts in the quick service area. Most Parts Managers pitch-a-fit when, it is suggested that, parts reside anywhere outside of their care and control. I contend that parts can be anywhere and still be under the care and control of the Parts Manager. Parts in the quick service area are simply assigned a different series of bin numbers.

Parts Managers who are especially worried about outlier inventories should set-up bi-weekly or monthly inventory accountability for the Quick Service Manager.

All parts should be assigned a part number, bin location, cost and list prices. OEM parts are priced by the DMS for the Dealer regularly. Parts that the

Parts Manager may have set-up for over-ride, non-factory parts or obsolete parts, are not priced. Your Parts Manager should have no problem setting up pricing and controls for a quick service operation. They should even be able to track all of the non-factory parts sold and offer stocking recommendations based on the ordering parameters of their DMS system.

The quick service operation should have full access to parts selling screens so that they can add parts to quick service repair tickets. This means, (paradigm shift again) that the Quick Service Advisor is, in effect, another parts counterman for the parts department. They will sell parts and add parts to their quick service inventories. This includes tires, filters, brakes, wiper blades and any other part that would be under the control of the Quick Service Advisor or Manager.

I have seen disasters where the parts department will not work with a quick service operation. They want to sell parts to the quick service business, like an outside vendor. The Parts Manager wants to declare gross profit on these parts before the quick service department sells them. This is regressive for the Dealer and will force the Quick Service Manager to seek parts from outside sources. Where is the gross for the Dealer in that?

Some Parts Managers are so controlling that they will only allow a very small inventory of parts to be warehoused in the quick service department. Of course this forces the quick service people to constantly be hanging out at the back counter of the parts department waiting on parts or, once again, buy parts from NAPA or some other supplier down the street. This does not work either.

Tires are parts that many Parts Managers don't really want to track. They are parts and they should have unique part numbers managed by the DMS inventory control system. Frequent stock orders should be pulled to gage movement on the fastest moving tire inventory and provide a guide when dealing with tire suppliers. Sure, all cost and list pricing will need to be done manually but you will have excellent records of what is selling and what is not.

What parts you choose to maintain in your quick service department should be determined by demand, just like your regular parts department. You should keep on hand; bulk oil, case oil products, lube products, air filters, oil filters and fuel filters for the brands your store represent. Brakes and batteries and wiper blades should be right there, easy to sell to your customers.

Visual display's and point of sale materials help move merchandise. You should consider some low cost alternatives for tiered maintenance parts pricing for your customers as well. A lot of dealerships sell wheels and accessories and retail clothing lines to balance out quick service. The only thing is, if it is a part, track it like a part and hold that part to sales accountability.

Quick Service Phones:

Separate phone service is absolutely critical for a quick service operation. You have a better chance of getting someone at the White House to answer your call, than you do in many new car dealerships. Being shuffled around by a receptionist whose only goal in life is to stop her phone from ringing is no answer for a customer calling to make an oil change appointment. Dealerships who employ answering machines are really telling their customers that the dealership has more important things to do than to talk with them. No one likes to talk to a machine.

Your quick service facility will need its own separate phone line. It is better to have an incoming phone line that rings directly to the quick service operation. A phone in quick service will siphon off all of those calls regarding appointments and price inquiries.

A phone in quick service will get a customer to the right person the first time. Most phone providers now offer a service where the phone will ring over to wireless phones when the phone rings more than 5 times or when the main line is busy. Calls forwarded will ring out to an Advisor, even if he is in a service bay with a Technician. ADP and Reynolds and Reynolds have a service where they will come into your dealership and perform a telephone survey for you and tell you your options.

 How many phones do you need? The quick service operation needs a direct phone line for regular business, a line for your DMS web based software and a line for credit card, check approval and maybe a line to check factory recalls and service bulletins. Do not route phones through the dealerships main switchboard. This will add to a communications bottleneck. If you are selling quick service to people with any make or model, what will they think when they get your switchboard?

It is important in a quick service operation to let your customers know that you are in business to serve them by using excellent phone service. The quick service operation will need a protocol for someone always answering the phone with-in three rings.

If your quick service employee is busy talking with a customer the phone call should transfer over to a real person who will pick up the call. When calls come into your sales department and the salesman is not available, who takes the message? I hope it is not an answering machine. Customers are like you, they want to talk to real people who will take a message. The flip side is that when messages are taken, it is vital to return them; otherwise your credibility is shot.

Uniforms:

When you choose to open a quick service facility it is important that you stick with a brand image. That brand may be yours or it may be that of a franchise but work the brand. Image not only covers the paint scheme and signage but it also means your employees need to look like they are ready to do business with your customers. Uniforms identify your employees to your customers when they come in to do business with you. Your quick service facility should have a uniform scheme different from those of your dealership employees. Golf shirts and logo shirts and a jacket in the winter worn by your quick Service Advisors will identify the customers to your brand.

Technician uniforms should carry the logo of your quick service facility as well. If you have employees dressed in what ever they choose to wear that morning, you may wind up with an embarrassing moment that you don't want to face. Uniform also means no visible tattoos and body piercing. You hire these people; you set the standard, have your employees live up to it.

Some parts of the country are far more formal than others. In the north east and the south east many managers wear shirts and ties when meeting customers. If that is the convention for your main shop, relax it a little bit for the quick service facility. These customers are in for maintenance services. You may be inviting them out into the shop to look at their vehicle, keep clothing friendly and business casual. I am not talking about plunging necklines on ladies and trousers that hang around well below legal limits. Let's face it, little old ladies come into get their oil changed, use some decorum.

Advertising and Marketing:

A quick service operation will need more aggressive advertising than in your regular service operation. You have a great advantage over competition down the road simply because you will get referrals from your new, used and service departments. You will begin to train your customers to return to you for all quick service maintenance items. This is your base and you will work it with a minimal advertising effort. If you expect to grow you will need to expand your business beyond this base.

Your competition attracts new customers through advertising. After market retailers use multi-colored inserts in every major newspaper in the country. They run block ads in the sports section every Saturday. They advertise in direct mail pieces, like Valpak. They will even advertise on radio and television and use just about any marketing scheme they can think of to capture your customers.

The aftermarket quick service operations use loss leaders to attract the attention of customers. Once they have the customer in the store they will employ a complete vehicle inspection and offer choices to the customer. In other words, they do a great job of up-selling.

Advertisement of this sort brings in people who are interested in the price point mentioned in the ad. When you engage in this activity you are in the conquest business, people who are not currently trading with you. You need to do this in order to build your business and hopefully be able to sell them a new vehicle down the road.

When customers receive a direct mail piece for tires they will walk out to their vehicle with the ad in their hand to look up the tire size on their vehicle and make a comparison. These same customers will carry the tire ad, from the paper or direct mail, into the tire store and point out what it is that they want. That is because these ads use tire price points. The ad lists mileage ranges of tires offered with a performance message. Tire sizes and a price are listed in the ad. The customer is responsible for multiplying the price times 4 to come up with an estimated cost. Somewhere in the ad there is also a cost for mounting and balancing, stems and valves. It does not matter that the ads are a little confusing, customers love them.

When you establish a quick service facility in a car dealership you will be creating a new identity for your business. You will be letting the public know that you can provide quick service with quality OEM and aftermarket parts for a fair price. Keep in mind that some things work better than others. Below are a few advertising points that do work:

Ad Campaigns that work:

- Direct mail works better than newspaper block ads. Direct mail is targeted and used to drive customers in the door with sales specials. Timing, frequency and cost control are the major considerations with direct mail. Direct mail is a conquest marketing tactic.

- Using your own computer, you can create your own hand bills and coupons. It is easy to print up a service special each month with coupons. Always print an expiration date on the document. These hand bills can be handed out to every main shop customer and every quick service customer. Hand bills can be distributed at public events and gatherings. Handbills can be handed to every customer who comes through your doors, even in your vehicle sales departments.

- Every time a customer comes in for service in your main shop or your quick service, always review their suggested maintenance and set a future appointment date with them. Then follow-up on these appointments and ask your customers to return.

- Take the time to visit your local professional office buildings. Offer a pick-up and delivery service to Lawyers, Doctors, business executives and their employees. People want to take their vehicles in for service but often they just do not have the time. Be convenient!

- When you print up tire prices, use the techniques mastered by tire stores. List tire price points and sizes with a single tire price. Go them one better and print the types of vehicles on which these OEM tires will fit.

- Place slow or no moving tires in local classified ads in your newspaper. Use Craig's List. Be sure to list what kind of vehicle the tires will fit on. People will make a quick connection if they think they can get a bargain for their vehicle.

- Advertise a "Lady's Day Special" in the Wednesday food section of the newspaper with a block ad. This is an attention getter. Make sure to stress quick, friendly service and the importance of a thorough vehicle inspection. Offer oil and filter changes with free tire rotations with an inspection. Do not use any acronyms or abbreviations and make it look like a clipper coupon that they can bring in. This advertising works! Once again this is conquest advertising.

- New owner clinics work. Some Dealers are sponsoring public safety meetings for young drivers, in conjunction with local law enforcement at the quick service facility. This is a great time to cover things like simple maintenance and how to change a tire in an emergency situation. This is a retention tool that keeps customers loyal.

- Another merchandising tool is to re-institute signing off in the customers' maintenance manual. If the customer does not have one, provide one for them. Provide some in-dealership value for the customer to trade-in their vehicle if they maintain it. A great company that offers custom dealer scheduled maintenance guides is

Mainstreet Marketing. They will print a scheduled maintenance book specific to your dealership. The books often have a trade-in coupon, good for money down on a vehicle, in the back. The customer is encouraged to maintain their vehicle in your dealership.

- Cross-merchandising with local vendors works. You offer them oil change or other service coupons and they offer you coupons for the movies, pizza discounts or what ever service or product they are selling. This quid pro quo keeps customers coming in the door. You hand out their coupons and they hand out yours. Great tool!

- Offer specials and discounts to churches and religious organizations. The way this works is if their members get their work performed at your business, you will set aside a small % of the sale into a fund that will be refunded to the church. The money is generally put into a building fund. They love this one and you get to deduct the money as a tax deduction to your business.

- Billboard advertizing is awareness advertizing. This works to alert local customers of your brand and what you offer.

Some advertising efforts are not as successful:

- Big tire sale events often do not work. They are attention getters and create awareness of your business operation but they are not too successful for improving traffic flow or selling services. Big events will often include a radio station remote, balloons, clowns, large inflatable tires and some food. This all cost money. On the other hand, if you tie a service event into a dealership vehicle sales event then perhaps you might get some bang for your buck. If you want to sell tires, price them right and use the other methods of advertising mentioned above.

- Weekly block ads in newspaper sports sections do not get read. An occasional ad is better than a weekly ad. All you gain from this type of advertising is more public awareness that you are in business. This does not generate much floor traffic.

- Radio and television are great awareness tools. TV lets people know who you are and what you do. It is doubtful someone will stop what they are doing and rush out the door to go buy that alignment special that you are offering, however. These ads are very expensive and will not drive floor traffic. You may have TV and radio accounts, for new vehicle sales campaigns, on which you can piggy-back a service ad.

I do know of one Service Manager in Tupelo, MS who used to bill himself as the Tire King. He ran radio ads two and three times a day and he sold a lot of tires because of it. His effort was extraordinary. Not everyone can pull off this type of campaign. If you can piggy-back on an ad that is already running, you can get your quick service message, (like "We sell tires!") out quicker. Otherwise, save your cash.

- Man with a sign. Hiring someone to walk up and down the street with a sign on them may get some people to make a snap decision and drive up for that quick oil change you are advertising. It may cause that customer to have an accident as well. You may be better served asking the local high school pep club to come onto your lot and wash customer's cars. You will definitely get more attention.
- NASCAR show cars, big wheel vehicles and things like them attract attention and will get people to drive onto your lot. You will get dads with their children but it is doubtful you will get much service sold for the effort. They are a great awareness tool though.

Internet Sales:

Wow! How much of our world is affected by the internet? Almost every person on the planet is "connected" in one way or another. Social networking is the order of the day. Facebook, Linkeden and other social networking outlets are all the rage. Someone in your dealership should be working on ways to maximize this attention getting media. This is a way to connect with younger buyers. Your message should be low key and informative. Let the younger buyers know that you are there to help them with their vehicle concerns, to answer questions, not just sell them something. That will go a long way to gaining loyalty from an up and coming generation who will be in their 30s before you know it.

Any time is a good time to capture the e-mail addresses of your customer base. When you do, send them e-mailed advertisements of service specials and maintenance reminders on a regular basis. These low cost friendly reminders do work. If there are coupons, people will print them and bring them in.

I know a Service Manager in Chicago who sends out an e-mail reminder to his customers every mid-winter to come in for his "Pot Hole Special." He offers a thrust alignment, coolant check and inspection for a low entry level price. Once the vehicle is in, they perform thorough inspections and make menu offerings. He does not have a January slump in business.

The internet works, but customers under 30 are busy sending text messages and twittering. That means you need to be capturing cell phone numbers in your computer as well. Ask for the best way to contact your customers when you write them up. Then ask if you can have their cell phone. The next question is, "Do you mind if we occasionally send bargains and specials to you by text?" Most will say "sure" because they have unlimited texting plans. Service reminders by text will net incredible results. Tweet or text your customers, to let them know that their repair work is complete. Tweet or text to let them know their parts are in. Tweet or text your customers, to thank them for their business.

What are you doing to advertise your Service department on your dealerships website? I have viewed hundreds of dealership websites and I have to tell you most need serious work. Your customers are checking you out on-line before they come in and buy. Your website needs to deliver the kind of information people are looking for.

When you click the box for Service on the typical dealership website, you are immediately asked to make an appointment. The viewer is faced with a series of boxes that want all of their personal information before proceeding. If you are like me, you cannot get out of that site fast enough. Dealerships are better served on their websites if they first display the friendly faces of their smiling employees. The other things that customers will want to look for are:

- What are the Hours of Operation?
- What are the Current Service Specials for this month?
- What Accessories are available for their particular make and model of vehicle and how much are they? Your Parts Manager is going to have to list prices and be prepared to transact business on the internet.

- What are the scheduled maintenance intervals and services for my particular make and model of vehicle?
- How much air should I have in my tires and where do I find this information?
- What are some safety tips on changing tires in an emergency?
- What does a check engine light indicate?
- A Reminder that your dealership is interested in providing a **Completely Satisfied Service Experience**. Then provide a comment section. The comments should be confidential.
- Some dealerships have an "Ask the Tech" Blog or e-mail access so that they can ask questions from a factory trained Technician. The most important concern here is to not to try to diagnose over the internet but to try to get the customer to come in and have a factory trained Technician look at the concern. These e-mail sites do allow people with basic questions to get some good answers.
- Finally, a way to make an appointment.

Personalization/Accessories:

Many Dealers would like to sell more accessories in their dealerships. The main reason they do not is that Sales Managers are convinced that once an accessory is introduced into a car deal they will have to sacrifice gross in order to compete with another possible Dealer down the road. Worse, they are afraid that they might have to give the accessory away. Dealers are also reluctant to pre-load accessories because they feel that they will loose their gross on accessories in a dealer trade.

Dealers will expect their salesmen to sell accessories and offer them incentives to do so. Some dealerships have a dedicated Accessory Salesperson speak with the customer before they go into F & I (Finance and Insurance department.)

The last ditch effort to sell accessories is to ask the F & I Manager to sell your accessories. By the time the customer gets to the F & I department they are generally ready to bolt for the door if one more thing is being offered to them. Some F & I Managers are quite good at offering these accessories but when they do, they may be sacrificing other menu items from the F & I menu.

Successful accessory selling Dealers simply pre-load the accessories and establish the base cost for their vehicle and expect their sales department to get the gross on top of the base. A smart Dealer knows that he is getting his gross on both, the accessory and the car deal.

Most dealerships will not preload, so they wind up trying to sell accessories through the parts department. When accessories do not sell, the parts become dusty idle inventory. Some Dealers eventually install these parts on used vehicles or wind up scrapping them. Bye, bye profit!

When you create a quick service facility you have the opportunity to establish an accessory and personalization boutique. This will allow you to offer and display accessories for your new and used vehicles in a separate environment from your new and used departments. The average truck buyer will spend $2,000 or more to personalize their vehicles, generally after they have purchased the vehicle. Customers buy up-graded music systems and radio equipment, chrome wheels, striping and decals, alarm systems, voice command phones, iPod interface, GPS, running boards, bug shields and everything you can imagine down to curb feelers, key chains and clothing lines. These popular items are just a few of the choices that a customer has from any accessory store down the road. The opportunity could be yours if you move into this market.

You can set aside a bay in a quick service department that performs this work with a dedicated accessory and personalization salesman and Technician. Some Dealers even prefer to have someone work in one of their bays on a contract basis. Accessories are another way to make you more money.

Hiring the Right People for Quick Service:

A quick service operation should have someone dependable in charge of that operation, a Quick Service Manager. They should also have an assistant to help run things when they are not around. Quick service operations need several Technicians, generally one or more for each service bay. This is the bare bones personnel requirement to get going.

Whether you choose to have your Quick Service Manager be a manager that reports directly to the General Manager or a store employee with the title who reports to your Service Manager is entirely up to you. There are advantages to structuring the chain of command both ways.

No matter whom they report to, Quick Service Managers are set up with their own performance goals, different from other dealership personnel. Often managers are hired from the aftermarket. A lot of them are former Firestone, Goodyear or WalMart employees. The difference in a dealership environment and where these managers came from is like day and night. Managers from aftermarkets make good employees. They work very hard and are used to the long hours.

The aftermarket is a great place to recruit personnel because they already know what to do to help make your business a success. You will find eager and willing candidates that see working in a new car dealership. To them it is like moving into the major leagues. Seek out Managers, Service Advisors and Technicians from this market.

When you prospect for personnel, in the aftermarket, you will offend no one, unless you happen to run into the business owner. When you walk into an aftermarket business, present your business card and tell them who you are. Tell them what you are trying to do and ask a few questions about how they operate. The conversation will get around to looking for people. Often you will be asked if you need someone. You will be surprised; many employees will jump at the opportunity to work in a car dealership.

I once approached an aftermarket Manager to see if he would want to work for one of my Dealers. I was surprised, when he told me that he could not afford the pay cut. Just because they work in the aftermarket does not mean they are all working for sub-standard pay.

Pay plans are different for people working in the aftermarket. Hourly pay and incentives may seem the same but shift work often cause a lot of stress. When they come to work for a new car Dealer they must make many adjustments that may seem uncomfortable for them. For example, dealership accountability and working with so many department Managers is confusing. To someone from the outside, the dealerships computer software is a nightmare. A dealership will have better hours of operation than where they came from and the employee benefits are much better.

When considering employees from the aftermarket quick service business, women are excellent choices. They are great at meeting and greeting customers and they put other women at ease. Women can defuse angry men easier than men and they do not try to diagnose problems for the customer. You can find mature women who can do this work in accounting offices, waiting tables in restaurants and selling furniture as well as the aftermarket. Mature women will demonstrate confidence and will appreciate the benefits package that you offer. They will need to learn how to present menus, ask the closing questions and they need to be willing to work the hours.

Recently retired men and women are good choices for employees, if they are looking for a new career path. You can advertise in church papers and local health facilities for this type of employee. They make excellent part time and shift employees to fill in for the extended hours in the quick service department.

Younger inexperience people are hip and attractive. You may get them cheaper but the turn-over is high. Remember, you are in the relationship building business when you deal in customer service. Still, a younger person will help you connect with your younger buyers.

When you hire a Quick Service Manager or Service Advisor, they should have access to both parts and service screens in your invoicing system and they should be responsible for handling cash. There needs to be a pay plan in place that encourages sales of both parts and labor, not just labor gross. There also needs to be some accountability for sending work to the main shop and for the shop to forward work back to the quick service facility.

A Quick Service Manager should be responsible for opening the doors in the morning and locking them up at night. The Quick Service Manager is also the main Service Advisor for write up and sales. This person should also be responsible for hiring and firing of Technicians. The Quick Service Manager is also responsible for managing work flow through his shop and keeping track of all tire and parts inventories.

The Quick Service Advisor/Manager is also the Cashier. This person will write-up the service ticket, up-sell the customer, hand the work to the Technicians, close the ticket, print it and collect money from the customer and close the ticket. Do not be afraid to trust them with this authority. Most transactions are credit card or check. Except for commercial accounts, you would be well advised to not put any quick service work on your dealerships accounts receivables.

The Quick Service Manager definitely needs an assistant who is also a Service Advisor. The assistants' job is to relieve the manager during the long hours required to operate the department. When business picks up you may even need to hire more Service Advisors to cover the traffic.

Some dealership quick service facilities are so large that they have an on-site parts person who dispenses parts to the Technicians. This person will keep track of the tire and parts inventories. Often they will shag parts from the dealerships parts department to the quick service department, delivering the parts directly to the Technician. This saves time and keeps the work moving through the quick service shop.

Your new quick service facility will offer opportunities for some of your existing employees to move into a new area of responsibility. New hires should have the opportunity to prove themselves in the quick service operation and then be able to move into a career path with-in the dealership. I always thought it was a good idea to rotate main shop Service Advisors in and out of the quick service department. This keeps them on their toes and stresses the need to be sharing work load with up-sells between departments. Service Advisors who occasionally work in the quick service department gain a new respect for how to treat your customers.

Quick Service Technicians:

Any quick service facility that handles maintenance and light repair will also need Technicians that will change tires, perform tire repairs, oil and filter changes and all fluid top offs. You will also need Technicians to be able to perform light repairs up to three hours billable time. In the quick service business you don't install tires without selling an alignment. This skill level will require more than what you will find in an oil change Technician. You will need to find good "B" and "C" level Technicians. You are not going to find Technicians, even entry level Technicians for minimum wage. If you do, you will not be satisfied with your results.

You want your Quick Service Technicians to spot other work on a vehicle that can be referred to the main shop. Oil and transmission leaks, unusual noises and air conditioning systems that do not work are all excellent opportunities for the main shop that your quick service may discover.

The one key difference between your main shop and a quick service operation is the customer is right there. You can take them right out to the vehicle to show them what work needs to be done. If the work is referred to the main shop, the Quick Service Advisor can help arrange transportation through a rental or a shuttle for the customer. A good "B" level Technician is capable of performing these tasks. Even though pay for most Technicians in the quick service is hourly, some Technicians are paid a flat rate with a bonus or spiff structure for finding and referring additional work.

A quick service facility is focused mainly on turning oil changes into multiple repair line tickets. The job in the quick service shop is to completely inspect every vehicle that comes through the operation. Every tire is inspected and every air filter is removed and shown to the customer. You not only want an employee who will inspect tire tread wear, look at rotors and calipers on brakes but you want them to be able to intelligently explain what they found to the customer. A Quick Service Technician may well be your best salesperson. Before you hire any employee, check their background thoroughly. Do not simply trust what is put on an application. Dig deep and call the references.

Pay plans and structure:

How you compensate quick service facility employees will determine the success of your operation. You definitely do not want to overpay them but they need to have an incentive base for your employees to build your business and make you money.

Quick service maintenance work has a lower gross than you may be accustomed to. You do not make as much money on an oil change and tire rotation as you do on a water pump replacement. A quick service business relies on volume and a lower cost of sale. Total sales, however, will look good, especially if you sell a lot of tires. The point is, you will need to compensate your employees with a combination of hourly wage and bonus incentives built in to perform the tasks of your quick service and meet your sales goals.

Compensation for a quick service manager should stress the operational goals of your business model. In other words, you will pay them differently than how you pay your Service Manager or Service Advisors in your dealership. Your profit goals can be reached if you set up pay plans that emphasize your performance sales objectives for volume and for customer satisfaction.

You want your Quick Service Advisors and Managers responsible for selling a great deal more maintenance and light repair than you are currently experiencing. You want them to keep your customers happy and returning on a regular basis so they will buy another vehicle from you. You want to keep the quick service clean and you want your employees working with minimal supervision. You want expenses kept under control. Pay the manager to do those things. Not just a dollar amount but specify what you want, set goals and pay accordingly for the performance.

Consider paying Quick Service Advisors on parts and labor sales, not gross. You want more volume. A focus on sales will make that happen. Parts sales should be a part of a Quick Service Technician pay formula as well. In most cases it is good to have a flat rate Technician or two along with hourly techs, especially if they are engaged in more complicated repair work. If you have a good "B" Technician on flat rate he just might take a shot at a CV Boot replacement or an AC repair on that off-brand vehicle. These are the Technicians who will become shop leaders and mentors to the other new hires. You will need to pay them a little more but not as much as a line Technician in the main shop.

Your main goal is to move volume through the quick service while making a profit. Make it work both ways. Install incentives for sending work to your main shop and incentivize your main shop employees for sending work to the quick service facility.

You should consider offering a mix of pay and incentives for Technicians. You will be able to hire entry level Technicians as well as experienced employees from other aftermarket operations for a quick service operation. In any market, you can expect to pay from $8.00 to $14.00 and hour for entry level Technicians. Offer them hourly wages with a stair step for performance goals that renew every week. Their hourly pay could go up each week based on how much they produce. Then they start over with their base wage at the beginning of each week.

Just as a side note: regardless of what your Office Manager tells you, never delay an incentive payment for any employee until the next month. If you engage in this behavior your incentive program becomes meaningless.

Other Opportunities for Income in Quick Service:

Once you have created your quick service facility you are only limited by your imagination where you want the business to grow. Some Dealers will start out with a maintenance and light repair facility and eventually morph them back into oil change shops. This is regressive. Your challenge should instead be to look at new opportunities and see where you can take them.

Consider possibilities like; selling Extended Service Contracts, offering Road Hazard Insurance, managing Car Rental, enrolling Credit Card applications, working with Fleet Service accounts, offering Pre-paid Maintenance packages, selling Personalization/Accessories (includes decals and striping), offering Detailing, selling Car Washes, performing Dent Doctor repairs, Radio and Electronic sales, GPS, Alarm system installation, Vehicle tracking chips, voice command cell phones, Used Vehicle reconditioning for your internals and performing internals for other Dealers down the street.

I know a Dealer who rented out one of his bays to some people on a contract basis to come in and do detail work. The service was so popular that when the contract was up he kept the signage and hired his own people to run the detail operation. On site and off site detail or retail detail is excellent money making tool. The choice is yours to make. In a smaller retail environment like a quick service operation you can offer services that would otherwise get lost in your main shop.

Measuring Quick Service Performance:

All of the following measurements are used to determine the success of quick service operations:

Parts and labor sales gross, Hours per repair order, Hours turned, Hours billed, Repairs per bay per day, Total sales per bay per day,

Gross Profit per bay per month, Gross Profit per Technician per month, Net profit per hours sold.

Measurements for measurements sake are no good and the numbers are no good if the only person looking at them is the Dealer. Measurements are tools to gage performance goals for improvement. They need to be meaningful, not some pie in the sky stretch goal, and they should be a part of a daily operational procedure. Every employee in a quick service facility should have visual access, daily, for what they are being held accountable. Posting their goals and achievements helps employees work to their potential.

A key performance goal in a quick service facility is how much work you are pushing through the shop in terms of dollars and cents. Two ways to measure this is; **average dollars sold per ticket** and **total sales per bay per day**. Since most of the work being performed is oil changes and tire rotations, it makes sense to tally total dollars as a guide. If you are measuring dollars sold, you will drive the low cost oil change and tire rotation to higher numbers. Dollars sold is an easy metric for any employee to calculate as they move through their work day.

Set incentives and contests based on sales. When the employee sells something, they know how that sale is going to impact their pay. Keep the math simple if you are interested in keeping your employees engaged in your business. If you have an incentive, pay the incentive now, not later. You loose your punch if you do not immediately reward success.

Patrick W. Emmett

CHAPTER 14

BUILDING A QIUICK SERVICE FACILITY

What Services to offer:

A quick service business should include oil and filter changes but in order to make money they also need to offer the following services:

- Complete vehicle inspections with every service
- Menu and bundle pricing packages to offer customers choices. Use mileage bands for services packages. Companies like BG and Wynns will offer excellent bundling and menu tools to help you.
- Tire sales and repair service. If you are planning on just doing oil changes you will not make enough to make your effort worthwhile. Tires are the number one defection repair for a customer. Tire sales work!
- Fuel filter, cabin air filters and air filters need to be offered on every sale.
- Brake services with good, better and best offerings for your customers.
- Alignments are critical for all tire sales. If you are in an area with pot holes, alignments make sense. Alignments are labor sales that add money to the bottom line.

- Flushes; engine, transmission, brake, power steering and coolant. These offerings make you money.
- Wheel and rim sales are vanity items that customers may want to add to a tire purchase.
- Shocks and struts are not easily sold. Take a cue from your competition. They will suggest shocks and struts after an alignment and anytime after 30,000 miles.
- CV Half Boots are another part that can be replaced as a result of an under the vehicle inspection.
- Batteries should be visually inspected for corrosion and always tested on vehicles over 30,000 miles.
- Wiper blades should be offered at every oil change. Customers want them to work right when they need them.
- Air conditioning maintenance services. Now you are getting into more skilled operations. "B" level techs can test and add coolant to an air conditioning system. Once you get into compressor issues the work then needs to go to your main shop.
- Simple component replacement on older model, non-house-branded vehicles, such as belts, hoses, water pumps and fuel pumps. All of this work can be performed in a quick service environment. You can use lower cost labor and aftermarket parts to remain price competitive.
- Your quick service facility needs an incentive to refer work to the main shop for write-up and the main shop needs an incentive to refer work to the quick service facility. They won't simply do it because it is the right thing to do. You need to make it worth their while.
- Nitrogen filling station - Keep customers coming back by having a Nitrogen filling station visible in your quick service work bays.

Any Dealer of any franchise can build a maintenance and light repair quick service business in or near their main facility. Re-engineering your building or adding something new is what we call a "brick and mortar" solution in the business. This means a capital investment. This investment is like a basic law of physics, **"it takes energy to make energy and it takes energy to move mass."**

Once you have made up your mind that a quick service facility is something you want to explore then you will need to consider these items:

- How much will it cost to get started?

- Will I need to build a new building?
- Just where would a quick service facility work in my dealership?
- How many bays would I need?
- Who would run it?
- What will my return on investment be?
- Why am I doing this again?

In any planning stage you must first get your facts together and develop a business plan. If you plan to borrow the money or expand your facility, most investors will request a 5 year Proforma to project earnings. This is done by making some hard decisions. First of all, how much are you willing to invest into a new business opportunity? If you are not willing to take that step, then save yourself the energy now and find something else to do with your time. There are plenty of people down the street from you who are willing to make that investment and they are doing so every day. It is your customers that will wind up in their shops.

How much money can I make?

In a dealership service shop, the average dealership will generate about $4-5,000 per month labor gross per service bay. This could be as much as $12,000 in total parts and labor sales per bay per month. The standard for a quick service operation is $8-10,000 in parts and labor sales per bay per month. That makes sense because you are selling work that is lower grossing than work in the main shop and you are only writing tickets that are under 3 hours of work. The main shop generates higher sales per bay because of the heavy work that is performed.

The average dealership sales of $12,000 per bay per month may not be your number. Earnings per bay in the main shop are frequently limited by the sheer number of oil changes that are performed at lower gross and the average of two bays per Technician that has become the standard in most shops.

Let's do a little math. If your average quick service ticket is $85.00 and you are selling just 5 repairs per bay per day in 5 bays and you are open 310 days a year then you can expect $658,750 in total sales per year. Service gross in a quick service is about 65% while parts gross is around 28%. These percentages can go up or down, depending on how many tires and aftermarket parts are sold. If your average gross for parts and labor combined is at 46% then your gross profit would be $303,025. As you can see there is great potential to make money with a quick service operation. The bottom line is you will be selling a lot more than an oil change and certainly a lot more than your people are currently doing out on your service isle today.

I have prepared a pro-forma calculation worksheet for you to use in Chapter 17. Manually plug in some of your own numbers, compare them with the pre-calculated formula for an 8 bay quick service business and see where the numbers take you. You may also contact me for a consultation concerning your plans. I can help provide you with a forecast on what expenses and profits might look like using different scenarios, for a fee, of course.

What should a Quick Service facility look like?

Quick service operations do best if there is a separate customer write-up area away from the main shop. Your quick service customers want to be written up quickly by people who are focused on why they came into your business. By separating the write-up your repair and warranty customers will feel like your Advisors are focused on their concerns as well.

In addition to the write-up area, quick service should also have a customer lounge that is separate from the main customer lounge. Quick service customers are all waiters and they are all looking for a positive maintenance experience. It is not wise to mix your warranty and heavy repair customers with these customers.

The customer lounge should to have its own restroom and refreshment area, separate from the main facility. Most waiting areas have a television and access to wireless internet. Some Lexus dealerships have a quiet room away from the main lounge for computer users and book readers. They have asked that people who use cell phones and the television people use a different lounge. Their customers seem to like it.

Any quick service operation needs to be identified with large clear signage that can be seen from the road. Directional signage in the dealership is sometimes used to point the way to and from your main shop write-up area. Signage and location are the most effective forms of advertising. Pick a good name for your quick service facility and proudly display it. Keep in mind that the name of your quick service facility should reflect who you are and what it is that you do.

Quick service operations should have parking in front of the write-up area. In this model, customers leave their vehicle, just like they do at Goodyear or Firestone store, and walk in for write-up. You gain vary little by having a drive through write-up. Your mission is to get the vehicle inside and on a lift rack for inspection.

Quick service operations should have pull-in and back-out service bays with a lift in every bay. At least one bay needs to be dedicated to alignments. If you are serious about commercial business you will need a larger lift and bay(s) to accommodate larger trucks and school busses. Many successful quick service facilities also offer a car wash.

How Big Do You Make a Quick Service Operation?

Dealers who have built Ford Quick Lanes repeatedly tell me, "I wish I had made it bigger, with more service bays." It is tempting and easy to under-build. The important thing to remember is that each bay you build is going to provide you with a monthly return on your investment. You are creating production space. If you think you need 4 bays, build 6. You will use all of them. If you think you need 6 build 8 and so forth. You won't be sorry. The difference in construction cost is minimal. If you are thinking of building anything less than 4 bays, think again! You simply will not get a decent return on your investment.

Service bays in your quick service shop should have plenty of overhead light. The floors should be exceptionally clean with tool boxes and work benches kept clean and free of anything that might embarrass the dealership. The Quick Service Manager needs to monitor this daily.

To be effective, you will want to invite your customers to come into the service bays. You will want to show them what their grooved rotor looks like on their car or the tread wear on their tires. You cannot have them tripping over shop rags and slipping on spilled fluids. This personal kind of interaction is what sells service and builds customer confidence. So when you are designing a building, consider a clear access to all service bays from the customer lounge. When you invite these customers out to the service bays they should always get a positive impression of cleanliness and order.

Your quick service facility will also need a storage area. The facility will need room for; oil storage tanks, compressor room, tire storage and tool storage and a place for your take-off tires that is out of customer sight. A parts storage area will be needed because your quick service Technicians cannot be running all of the way over to the main shop back counter every time they want a part.

If you choose to add a car wash there are many choices available for you. Broadway, Ryko and D&S are just a few of the companies that can help you get started. Customers do like to keep their cars clean. Getting a clean car when you get service makes you feel better about the money you just spent on maintenance. Works every time! Car wash facilities are either a cash cow or a money pit depending on what kind of equipment you buy and how well it is maintained. Shop around. There are some pretty good companies out there who have complete turn-key car wash packages for a reasonable cost.

Make sure you have a write-up area and customer lounge with clear visibility into the quick service shop. Customers want to watch the work being performed on their cars. Make sure that you have glass that meets local fire and safety standards between the customer lounge and the service bays.

Where to build a quick service facility:

After you have decided what you want your facility to look like you will need to make a choice as to where it will be. Where you place your facility will probably depend on where you can find the space. You have three choices: on-site, stand-alone on your dealership lot and off-site.

On-Site:

Do you have room inside of your existing facility? Today, many Dealers are under capacity and they have extra space. If you do, can you re-design your facility to accommodate a separate write-up area with customer lounge and restroom?

What are the draw-backs and what are the advantages? I was working with a Dealer in Louisiana on building a Quick Lane. The Dealer had made the decision to go ahead with construction in a building next to the dealership. We had a plan developed and we were ready to proceed when the contractor informed us that in order to have a customer lounge, the Dealer would need to tear up 30 feet of concrete in the shop floor to reach the sewage pipes at the back of the building. This was a roadblock but not a deal breaker. The Dealer chose to put the pipe in and go ahead with construction. I have spoken to this dealer many times and he has never regretted his decision. Sometimes you have to make adjustments. That's what this Dealer did.

Many Dealers make the choice to use existing service bays in the shop, former body shop or get-ready department to construct a quick service facility. Some choose to increase capacity by building additional production stalls adjacent to the existing shop with an add-on building.

Often, the least expensive solution is to convert existing space into a separate operating facility under the same roof. I have seen all solutions; re-work the existing shop space, a metal building add on to the main shop, a free standing metal building next door, move into an existing building across the street and one Dealer even converted an old church that was next door into a quick service facility. Every dealership is different, requiring study before you begin.

Conversion of existing stalls may require that you sacrifice existing labor producing bays. In most shops there are several flats or stalls without lifts in them. Efficiencies may be gained by increasing the lift count in the shop and eliminating the flats. Flats are a luxury.

Where and how are PDI and get-ready being done, and by whom? Does your facility have wash bays and stalls that simply store equipment and tools? These may provide additional opportunities for expansion. If you take a sharper look at how your shop and parts departments work they may be re-engineered to provide a better use of space. What ever you do, keep in mind that your quick service facility should be easy to find, have adequate parking in front of it and enough space to do the work.

Wherever you build, you need to keep a couple of things in mind. The first is what are the environmental requirements for drainage and storage of hazardous waste? If you are converting your existing shop you may already have this covered. You will also need to consider the addition of a restroom in a customer lounge. How is the space that you are looking at going to accommodate this addition? A plumber will be able to help you with this and tell you how drainage and access to water and electricity will work.

Conversion of existing space:

Many Dealers see conversion of existing space in their dealerships as the quickest and least expensive option to adding a quick service segment to their shop. The cost of converting existing facilities varies greatly. Local contractors sometimes can provide not only a cost of construction estimate but they can also draw-up the plans and submit them to your local zoning and planning commissions for you. Your local codes will determine if you must use an architect or if you can use contractor plans.

When converting existing space, the temptation is to scale back and save money on construction costs. Do not sacrifice service bays in your construction plans. Service bays bring you money. Bringing customers to the service bays is an important part of a successful formula, and a well organized customer lounge are important, so don't cut here.

Be frugal but plan ahead for the future. For most Dealers though, adding onto an existing dealership or converting existing space is the better solution for the maximum benefit, as long as it is not done half-heartedly. Using existing facilities will give you your fastest return and recovery on investment.

Building a new stand alone facility:

Dealers build a stand alone facility for many reasons. Perhaps they have several vehicle lines they are trying to accommodate in their main facility. The dealerships main facility may not lend its self to a quick service retail environment. Other Dealers see combining their Used Vehicle operation under the same roof as the quick service business. Whatever your reasons, you will have a great deal of flexibility with what your building will look like.

Building from the ground up is the best of all possible solutions because you are not trying to adapt a space that may not have been designed for something else. You can build a lot of things into a new facility like an isle down the middle of the service bays for customer access or an attractive write-up area. You can build as many service stalls as you want and room for plenty of storage. You can even include a car wash.

Contractors will tell you that it is easier to build up to date fire, plumbing and electrical requirements while a building is under construction than it is to adapt an existing older facility to current code. In other words, it may be cheaper to build from the ground up.

When you build a stand alone facility you are planning for the long run. Your return on investment will take more time. This is the same formula that your competitors use down the street only you have the advantage of owing existing prime real estate. Take a good look at that Goodyear. How many service bays do they have? When you build a stand alone facility, you have many options that might not exist in your main dealership facility.

Off-Site Quick Service facility:

When you choose to go off-site to a property down the street, you are changing the business model. The main purpose of building a quick service facility at a car dealership is customer retention. The second key reason is to sell more service and make more money by shifting work between the main shop and the quick service facility. The third reason is to look at additional dealership profit opportunities like accessory sales and car rental that can be managed out of this space. When you move down the road you loose some of that. You move from the customer retention model to the customer conquest model.

An off site facility will truly be an all makes and all models one stop shop. With the customer conquest model you will need to focus on constantly trying to drive new business through the door. Your competition does this successfully every day, so this is still a very good model. If you do no warranty work and you display no automobile manufacture signage on the property then you probably would not need to seek any permission from your franchising auto manufacturer. What you are doing is creating a separate business opportunity down the street. Building an off site facility would be no different than if you opened a Krispy Kreme franchise or moved your body shop.

I have known Dealers who were able to buy a turn-key quick service operation down the street or across town at real bargain prices. There are many advantages to doing this. First of all; once the ink is dry you are in business. Second, you do not have all of the construction and development concerns. You still have the option to re-engineer the facility with signage and paint to call the business your own. There are a couple of draw backs. You will find it more difficult catering to your customer base the way you want to. The person you bought the business from may have been happy earning a lot less from his operation than you would be. After all, he did sell the business. You would need to make significant changes in how business is performed. You might be letting yourself in for more problems than were obvious from the outside.

Another reason for going off site is the desire to expand into a satellite used car operation. If you build a quick service facility or convert an existing building at another location, you are opening up new opportunities to make more money. I know one Dealer in Alabama that went off site with a new facility to house both a used car department and a quick service facility. He even chose to incorporate a car wash. All three operations are a success as a stand alone investment. The money he makes on this lot is shown on a separate financial statement. He has a combined financial statement that shows these earnings as other income. Since the Used Vehicle operation is not part of his dealerships franchise business he was in no conflict with his manufacturers' sales and service agreement.

CHAPTER 15

COST OF CONSTRUCTION

Cost of Construction:

You probably have some pre-conceived idea as to how you want your quick service facility to look. Unless you just buy someone else's business you will have to engage in some form of construction.

Construction per square foot varies wildly from coast to coast. In your area the average cost of construction may only be $45 per square foot in other areas it is as much as $350 per square foot. The average nationally is about $135. If you build a 6 bay 50 X 75 (3750 Sq foot) building, your estimated average cost of construction would be $506,250.

If you convert existing bays in a facility and the construction is for a customer lounge and parts storage then you might be looking at construction on 800 square feet or less. That would put construction at $108,000 using $135 per square foot.

Once a building is constructed, you still need to pave the lot, put up building signs and directional signage. The business will need 6 or more lifts, one of which needs to be an alignment rack. You will need; tire changing equipment, lift racks, tire storage racks, furniture, fixtures and tire and parts inventory. You can easily invest from $100,000-$800,000 in equipment and fixtures to build and open a new quick service facility. Equipment could be shifted from the service department. The parts department may already have tire inventories and they will be able to supply the maintenance parts needed. There are several ways to gain some economy and lower the cost of your initial investment.

These numbers are not meant to discourage you. If you were to open a franchised operation like a McDonalds your estimated investment could easily reach 2-5 million dollars. A stand alone Valvoline or a Pennzoil franchise, on key real estate, has requirements could easily require 1 million dollars or more. Before you make any decisions, put a pencil to all of the numbers and do what makes sense for you.

The best method is to take all of your construction costs and operating expenses against forecasted earnings in a 5 year model. A 5 to 10 year profit projection will give you your best picture as to whether your money will be well spent or not. Who doesn't want an instant return on their money?

A quick service operation is a long term investment. A 5 bay quick service model could easily give you between 25-50% return on investment over 3 years or less. You will not easily find that in the stock market these days. The earnings potential is limited to your imagination and your quickest return will be realized in greater production from your main shop. You will make money with the opportunity to up-sell customers in a positive, maintenance oriented environment. Dealers who have made this choice are not disappointed.

Basics for the design and construction of your facility:

- You will need fire safe glass to separate the customer lounge and the shop area. You will need to get this signed off on by your local fire marshal.
- You should use an industrial, non-slip tile in the customer write-up area. This is critical from a law suit stand point. Do not use carpet, it is too difficult to maintain and it looks bad after a short period of time.
- Your restrooms and waiting lounge will need to be wheel chair accessible and must have tile floors that meet industrial code.
- Plan on customers parking in front of the service area with your customers walking into the building for write-up. Drive-throughs are a waste of space and manpower.
- Keep colors muted and soft. You do not need contrasting orange and black to stand out. Your great service will do that for you.
- Organize your point of sale displays and display fixtures so that they do not crowd the customer waiting area. Customers need to feel comfortable and welcome, not overwhelmed. Design space for point of sale materials in your initial floor plan. Make your room large enough. You could easily have for up to 30 waiters on a Saturday.
- The write-up area should be friendly to the customer. Remove barricades and walls like huge write-up desks and counters. If you must build a write-up desk, build them low and turn them around so that the write-up screens are visible to the customer. Round tables where customers can sit and discuss their needs are a far better environment for making decisions.
- Install a direct phone number and line into the quick service facility. You want your customers to call and set-up appointments, with-out going through the main dealership receptionist desk.
- Provide an area where small children can be entertained. We are not talking about Disneyland here just a TV and/or a Lego table.
- A space should be set aside for refreshments. Coffee, soda pop and vending machines are common.
- Customers need visual aids to make clear buying decisions. Tire cutaways, worn break pads, dab a lube displays, worn shocks and battery point of sale items need to be in a clear and easy to use area for the quick service advisors.
- Tires need to be everywhere. The place needs to smell like new rubber.

- If you are trying to appeal to all makes and all models; you are wise to keep the manufacturers logo out of the write-up area. If the quick service operation is at your dealership, the customer knows what brand of vehicle you sell. All customers need to feel comfortable bringing their off-brand vehicles in for quick service.

- Name your quick service facility. Build a brand that is tied to your dealership, not necessarily the factory unless you are building a factory quick service program.

- There is a debate over oil pits vs. lifts. Jiffy Lube and others use an oil pit. You cannot rotate tires easily and provide as many additional maintenance procedures over a pit. You cannot align a vehicle on a pit. Bays with lifts are the best solution for most Dealers and are less expensive than a pit.

- Detailed repair estimates should be provided to every customer before work begins in the shop. The customer will sign the work order to approve the work. This is a procedural thing but many Dealers forget this step. So you will need room for printer, fax machine and some computer hardware.

- A place should be set aside as an employee area. Some Dealers build a separate Quick Service Managers office, others simply have a room for employees to eat in. You should have an area to display daily sales measurements and who sold what. Quick service employees need to see targets and goals to keep them on their game.

CHAPTER 16

THE MYSTERY SHOP

Earlier in the book I recommended that you go out and mystery shop your competition. I put this chapter in the book because; this process should be performed by all Dealers, even if they do not build a quick service facility.

There are two ways to mystery shop. One way to do your mystery shopping is by phone. Call your competition. Ask who ever answers various questions from a prewritten script. The second way is to actually visit the site where you interview employees and take notes. Both methods are useful and each will yield different results.

You can actually hire several different companies who would be glad to provide you with everything you want to know on a regular basis about your competition. These companies are good at what they do and they will bring you thorough results, in graph form, for a price.

I know several dealerships where they have a chalk board posted in the service isle. The numbers are clearly visible, so customers can read the results. The board lists specific labor operations and a posted price of competition from down the street. These boards are updated weekly and the Service Advisors will use the boards to close customers who are balking on price. Some dealerships have a meet or beat policy for "apples to apples" repair work. Some dealerships offer meet or beat pricing for all tire sales. Chalk boards are just a merchandising tool that works, but to make it work you need to know what the other guys are selling their products for.

Customers come into your Service department now with pre-conceived notions as to how much a particular service might cost. Often they have called around before they came in to your shop and they showed up hoping to negotiate a discount. Your Service Advisor are at a disadvantage, right off. They don't know if the customer is lying or what the competition is really offering for the price.

If brakes were your customers concern, your competition probably offers a "one size fits all" brake pad replacement for a loss leader. The price quoted by the competitor, typically will not include calipers or turning the rotors. The work is more than likely being performed by an unskilled Technician. But your Advisor does not know any of this.

Advisors are at a distinct advantage if they can point to a price board and compare your price to the exact same service as the competition. In order to be in the price ball park, they would then offer the customer a choice between; OEM, Value Price Factory and Aftermarket options. The customer has all the information they need. They will have no reason to shop anywhere else.

Find out how much the competition charges for their services that you are both offering. Dig into what kind of parts they use. You will discover this and much more with a mystery shop.

The Phone Shop:

Before you begin to call your competition you should first consider phone shopping your own dealership. Ask a family member or friend to make the

146

call for you. Your employees probably know what your voice sounds like. Find out exactly what your customers are hearing when they call your business. Ask the same questions that you will ask the competition and find out what your results are.

Aftermarket visit:

As I have stated in previous chapters, do not be afraid to walk into your competitors businesses down the street. I understand that car Dealers are high profile in their community and might not want to actually make the visit themselves. In that case, use a family member or even an employee. Send them in to have some service performed. This person can ask any question that you might ask.

The survey that I provided is a place to start. You may want to take note of any services they may have posted and how much they are charging. If you ask, they will tell you what kind of parts that they are using. In most cases these will be one size fits all makes and models parts.

Pay special attention to the hours of operation. Is the place clean and welcoming to customers? What is the layout of the floor plan? Is there easy access to service bays? A visual inspection of the business is always much better than a phone interview.

You don't go into battle without good intelligence. Be prepared go armed with a talk track and a check sheet. I have prepared two work sheets for you to use. You will probably modify and use your own. The only rule is to be consistent.

Quick Service Mystery Shop Example

Phone Shop:

Call local service businesses in your area. Tell who ever answers the phone that you are seeking a brake job on a late model vehicle. Give them the make, model. For example, "I am looking for a brake job on my 2008 Chevy Cavalier. How much do you charge?" Then see what they say.

Date:_____   Name of Business: _____

Town: _____   Phone Number: _____

Who did you speak to? _____

How were you greeted?_____

Did they ask how you knew the breaks were bad? Y/N _____

Did they ask how many miles were on the vehicle? Y/N _____

Did they use automotive jargon without adequate explanation; turn the rotors, R&R the rotors, pads, calipers? Y/N _____   Provide instructions on how to find their business? Y/N _____

Did they ask you for an appointment? Y/N _____   Did they diagnose on the phone? Y/N ____

What price(s) did they quote? $_____ $_____

Comments:_____

_____

_____

How would you rate this experience with 10 being the best? _____

If you are price shopping different services, use different callers for your list of services.

QUICK SERV

Quick Service Mystery Shop Visit Example

Mystery Visit:

Date:_____   Name of Business: _____

Who greeted you?: _____ How Quick?: _____

What Services does this business offer?: Oil ___ Tires ___ Brakes ___ Wash ___

Flushes ___ Filters ___ State Inspections ___ Alignments ___ Nitrogen ___ Batteries ___

Light Repair Services? _____

Heavy Repair Services? _____

Do they have a menu visible? Y/N ____ Do they have Good/ Better/ Best choices? Y/N ____

If this is an oil change facility, how many people on the service isle? _____

Do they have lifts _____ or pits_____? What kind of parts? _____

Can you watch the work being performed on your car? Y/N ___ Is the place clean? _____

Is their a customer lounge? _____ Is their a bathroom near the customer lounge? _____

If an oil change, did the tech show you your dirty air filter? Y/N ____Did you buy one? Y/N ___

Comments   about   this   business:

_____

_____

_____

How would you rate this business with 10 being the best? _____

Price notes: _____

Patrick W. Emmett

CHAPTER 17

A SAMPLE QUICK SERVICE PROFORMA

The Proforma Worksheet:

I have included a first year Proforma worksheet for you to review with this book. I use a worksheet like this one, when I consult with Dealers to forecast what their projected expenses and return on investment would be. The beauty of the worksheet is working "what if" scenarios to find the right investment fit for a Dealer. The worksheet also has a break-even point to let you know what minimum performance would be as well. The formulas can even be expanded and worked into a 5 year business plan, providing an operational roadmap as to where the business should grow.

The worksheet looks at a typical 6 bay quick service model. This model has an estimate of construction costs and a break down of average operating expenses. Using the pre-suggested numbers to guide you, write out some predictions in each category as to what you think your initial investment would be then apply the operating expense numbers to your plan. This pencil to paper effort will give you some idea what kind of a gross profit you can shoot for.

Annual Forecasted Operating Expenses

	Dollars	Your Number	% of Sales
Technician Pay (Cost of Sale)	$163,448		18.5%
Sales Expense			
Management/General Service	$85,000		9.6%
Advertising and Promotion	$12,234		1.4%
Training	$3,534		0.4%
Policy Adjustment	$1,767		0.2%
Shop Tools and Supplies	$2,651		0.3%
Vacation Pay (if applicable)			0.0%
Other			0.0%
Total Sales Expense	**$105,186**		
Fixed Expenses			
Administration	$884		0.1%
Employee Benefits	$37,991		4.3%
Payroll Taxes	$34,457		3.9%
Retirement	$0		0.0%
Rent/equivalent	$35,000		4.0%
Real estate taxes	$6,796		0.8%
Utilities	$5,437		0.6%
Telephone	$4,418		0.5%
Permits and fees	$1,000		0.1%
Insurance	$1,359		0.2%
Office/Sales Supplies	$816		0.1%
Professional fees	$952		0.1%
Data Processing/Computers	$2,583		0.3%
Interest - equipment	$0		0.0%
Accruals - equipment	$0		0.0%
Interest - signs, furniture, fixtures	$0		0.0%
Accruals - signs, furniture, fixtures	$0		0.0%
Depreciation - equipment/tools	$7,700		0.9%
Depreciation - signs, furniture, fixtures	$2,100		0.2%
Equipment maintenance	$680		0.1%
Building maintenance	$952		0.1%
Miscellaneous expense	$5,000		0.6%
Total Fixed Expense	**$148,124**		
Total Expenses	**$253,309**		

Annual Forecasted Operating Expenses (page 2)

	Your
	Number

Facility Planning

Total Quick Service sq ft	3800
Renovated square foot - Construction	3800
Rent on facility to dealership	$10
Construction for new per sq ft (est.)	$130
Renovation estimate	$494,000

Estimate of total sales

Number of bays	6
Average RO's/bay/day	5
Total Repair Orders per day	30
Number of days open/year	310
Total Repair Orders per Year	9300
Average dollars parts/labor per RO	$95
Total Parts/Lab Sales Forecast	$883,500
Gross as a % parts and labor sales	46%
Gross on parts and labor sales	$406,410

Initial Investment

Construction Cost - est.	$494,000
Equipment/Tools - est.	$110,000
Computer Equipment	$7,000
Signs, Furniture & Fixtures	$18,000
Estimated additional Tire Inventory	$14,000
Additional Parts inventory	$14,000
Total initial Investment	$657,000
Net Return on Investment	23.3%

Return on Sales

Average annual total Sales	$883,500
Gross Profit	$406,410
less Total Sales Expense	$105,186
Selling Gross	$301,225
less Total Fixed Expense	$148,124
Profit before tax	**$153,101**
Return on Sales	17.3%

Patrick W. Emmett

Annual Forecasted Operating Expenses (page 3)

Break Even Analysis	
Total Sales and Fixed Expenses	$253,309
Gross as a % of Sales	46%
Annual sales to break even	**$550,672**
sales per day to break even	**$1,776**
sales per stall per day to break even	**$296**
Average dollars per Repair Order	$95
Total annual RO's to break-even	5797
RO's per stall per day to break even	3

CHAPTER 18

QUICK SERVICE VENDOR LIST

I wanted to provide a place for you to start in your quest for more information on how to go about building a quick service facility in your dealership.

I have dealt with most of the vendors listed but the list in this book is not a specific endorsement of any product or service. These businesses can be of some assistance and a good place to start.

When it comes to matters such as looking for quick service software, you should always first consider your existing Dealer Systems Provider (DMS). Find out what assistance they can give you to help set up your quick service as a separate profit center in your dealership. Some Dealer Systems Provider's are more helpful than others so keep in mind that there are many consultants out there that can work with your dealership's system administrator to make the changes.

Oil Company distributors are very helpful as well. Many such as Pennzoil, Valvoline and Castrol Oil have franchise programs that could fit very nicely into your quick service model.

Finally, your automobile manufacturer of the brand(s) of cars that you represent will have a considerable amount of advice on what vendors you should use. Use good judgment and shop around.

Quick Service Vendor List

Design/Build:

Customer Facilities, Inc.   317-259-6638

6296 Rucker Rd. Suite C   www.customfacilities.com

Indianapolis, IN 66220

DBM – Design Build Management   886-467-4900

18330 Fitzpatrick Lane   www.db-m.com

Occidental, CA 95464

Facility Design Services inc.   770-992-8801

10903 Alpharetta Highway   www.facilitydesignservices.com

Roswell, GA 30076

Omniplan Automotive Retail Facility Planners   905-434-5411

2000-D 1748 Baseline Rd. West   nfo@omniplangroup.com

Courtice, OT L1E 2T1

QUICK SERV

Equipment:

Challenger Lifts

200 Cable St.

Louisville, KY 40206

800-648-5438

www.challengerlifts.com

Eagle Equipment

4810 Clover Rd.

Greensboro, NC 27405

800-336-2276

www.eagleequip.com

Hunter Equipment

11250 Hunter Dr.

Bridgeton, MO 63044

313-731-3020

www.hunter.com

National Auto Tools

814 Blue Mound Rd.

Ft Worth, TX 76131

866-563-5438

www.nationalautotools.com

Panther Lifts

P.O. Box 2018

Cleburne, TX 76033

866-665-4387

www.pantherlifts.com

Rotary Lifts

2700 Lanier Dr.

Madison, IN 47250

800-640-5438

www.rotarylift.com

Tires:

Bridgestone-Firestone	800-367-3872
P.O. Box 7988	www.bridgestone-firestone.com
Chicago, IL 60680	

Continental-General	www.generaltire.com

Goodyear	267-468-6201
1144 East Market St.	www.goodyear.com
Akron, OH 44316	

Michelin Tire Co.	866-866-6605
1 Parkway S.	www.michelinman.com
Greenville, SC 29615	

TCI Tire Distribution Centers	864-329-2700
310 Inglesby	www.tirecenters.com
Duncan, SC 29334	

Uniroyal	877-864-7692
P.O. Box 19001	www.uniroyal.com
Greenville, SC 29602	

Toyo Tire a& Rubber	West Coast 800-442-8696 East Coast 800-444-8696
6261 Katella Ave.	www.toyotires.com
Cypress, CA 90630	

QUICK SERV

Tires:

Yokohama Tires, USA   800-722-9888

601 S. Acada Avenue   **www.yokohamatire.com**

Fullerton, CA 92831

Nitrogen:

NitroFill   954-970-1691

2160 Park Central Blvd. N.   www.nitrofill.com

Pompano Beach FL 33064

PurigeN98   954-383-7546

523 Sawgrass Corporate Pky   www.purigen98.com

Sunrise, FL 33325

Quick Service Software:

Alldata   800-697-2533

9412 Bighorn Blvd.   www.alldata.com

Elk Grove, CA 95758

Tire Guru – ABMS   877-470-2267

895 N. Main   www.tireguru.com

Logan UT 84321

Signage:

Bell Signs, Inc.   800-868-0284

1200 Bell Ave.   www.bellsigns.com

Panama City, FL 32401

Signage:

National Signage Affiliates   800-354-6416

109 Chappareal   www.nationalsignageaffiliates.com

Corpus Christi, TX 78403

Car Wash:

Broadway Equipment Co.   1-800-328-7434

4701 Humboldt Avenue North   www.broadwayequipment.com

Minneapolis, MN 55430

Ryko Manufacturing Co.   515-986-3700

1500 SE 37th. St.   www.ryko.com

Grimes, IA 50111

Flush Equipment:

BG Products, Inc.

704 S. Wichita   www.bgprod.com

Wichita, KS 67213

Wynns   1-800-989-8363

1050 W. Fifth St.   www.wynnusa.com

Azusa, CA 91702

Employee Screening:

Management By Strengths, Inc.   913-393-2525

601 N. Mur-Len/ Suite 16   www.strengths.com

Olathe, KS 66062

Petrochemical companies:

Amoco
Chevron
Conoco
Dow Chemical
Dupont
Enron
Imperial Oil
Kerr-McGee Corporation
Litton Industries, Inc.
Mobil Oil
Motorola
Mutual Life of Canada
Nova Corporation of Alberta
Occidental - Chemical Division
Occidental - Oil and Gas Division
Phillips Petroleum Company
Rhone Poulenc
Syncrude

ABOUT THE AUTHOR

Patrick W. Emmett is an Automotive Dealer Consultant who has over 30 years of experience in the automobile business working with car dealers. He offers advice on how to better manage car dealership Parts and Service departments. While at Ford Motor Co. Pat worked on the Quick Lane project to help build better customer service experiences for owners of Ford products. After Ford Motor Co. Pat worked with Don Reed of Dealer Pro Training Solutions and later at NCM Associates as a Dealer 20 Group Moderator. He has used that experience to consul car dealers of all brands on how to create a quick service department for their dealerships. Pat frequently speaks before automotive dealer groups and works with dealers to improve Parts and Service department gross profits..

Pat is author of the book, A Second Chance, Surviving Sudden Cardiac Death and is the Chairman of the Heart of America Sudden Cardiac Arrest Association. He is frequently invited to be a guest speaker at dinner meetings and heart health conferences from coast to coast. He is married with three adult children two grand children and lives in Overland Park, Kansas.

QUICK SERV

www.ingramcontent.com/pod-product-compliance
Lightning Source LLC
Chambersburg PA
CBHW051519170526
45165CB00002B/535